This book is a passionate plea for authenticity in entrepreneurship. Entrepreneurship that assures flourishing, creative organizations. Organisations that are real, that you want to belong to.
Use the stories and the atmosphere of this book to make your own organization more fun and more aware of its place in modern society.

Get out of your straight jacket and go for it!
Rip off your neck tie and dance....

Leen Zevenbergen.

Apart from any fair dealing for the purpose of research or private study, or criticism or review, as permitted under the Copyright, Designs and Patents Act 1988, this publication may only be reproduced, stored or transmitted, in any form or by any means, with the prior permission in writing of the publisher, or in the case of reprographic reproduction in accordance with the terms and licences issued by the Copyright Licensing Agency. Enquiries concerning reproduction outside those terms should be addressed to the publisher. The address is below.

Global Professional Publishing Limited Ltd
Random Acres
Slip Mill Lane
Hawkhurst
Cranbrook
Kent TN18 5AD

© Leen Zevenbergen 2011

The moral right of the author has been asserted.
All rights reserved. No part of this book may be reproduced in any form or by any means without permission in writing from the publisher, except by a reviewer who may quote brief passages in a review.

ISBN: 978-1-906403-69-0

Printed by Butler Tanner & Dennis Ltd

For full details of Global Professional Publishing titles in Finance, Banking and Management see our website at:
www.gppbooks.com

RIP OFF YOUR NECKTIE AND DANCE

LEEN ZEVENBERGEN

Creatively entrepreneurial and thrillingly inspirational

GLOBAL
professional
publishing

Creative

12	Narrow Minds & Rigid Strategies
16	Creativity — having a ball
22	You want to play?
27	How about doing nothing for a change?
32	The beauty of flow
37	Chaos and order
42	Nightmares as a recipe for a good night's sleep
50	The Myth of Innovation

The Great Adventure

56	From Dreaming to Doing
60	Scary stuff — starting a company
66	The Fun of Starting a Venture
70	Where is the market?
74	Don't forget the customers
82	Hey, Buddy: Get me some new business
88	Managers and entrepreneurs

6	Rip off your necktie and dance (Foreword)
218	And thanks
220	Books Consulted

Sparkle!

96	Business Dialogues
100	Enjoying the job
104	Happiness and happy organizations
110	Big organizations, can also radiate
116	Survival of the Happiest Happy Campers
120	The House of Fun
124	Enjoying, not so easy!
130	Sparkling and touching
134	An entertaining dinner party, sir

Inspire

140	Four professionals had a dream
144	Inspiring Organizations
150	What do you do without dreams?
156	Who has a vision?
161	Leadership or hardship
166	The conscious company
170	Real people
176	Synchronism stays surprising
180	How about doing something for the world?

AND WHAT NOW?

186	
191	Long live anarchy!
198	After all, it's your own business
204	Sparkling in a split second
211	We're going to travel

Rip off your necktie and dance

Before you can put your personal vision down on paper, you have to throw a switch. You have to whip off your tie, put your feet on the desk, and let the five o'clock shadow start growing on your clean-shaven image. Before you know it, you'll start feeling a lot more creative. If you're a woman, of course, you'll find another route to stirring up your creative juices. But you get the point. The point is: do whatever it takes to get out of the mindset that has kept you in a box.

Let me start with an essential question. Are people really happy at their jobs? Or with their jobs? Research shows that very few people are interested in the goals of the organization they work for. Why is it that people often come alive the minute they leave the workplace, whether it's an office or a factory? And that it's only after-hours that creativity starts bubbling up in all sorts of ways. At the fitness center, for example, or the billiard or bowling club, or a meeting of the PTA, or when a person starts planning to launch his or her own business.

Are we living in a time when on-the-job creativity is really appreciated? Or is creativity regarded as a nuisance, or worse, as actually counterproductive? Is innovation seen as essential for the continued existence of the business concern? Or is it regarded as a necessary evil?

Recently I spoke with a group of top managers of large concerns who were using an expression that was new to me. They were talking about a loincloth project. A loincloth project is one that management doesn't want to take on, but feels obliged to in order to show that it's responding to some social issue or problem.

Companies come up with all sorts of so-called innovative, creative, inspirational projects, if you look into the heart of management, you'll find that truly innovative projects are not supported by the top executives. They are not deeply rooted or thought through. And thus they lack the support of top management. How can a leader inspire if he or she is totally uninspiring? Not by generating a loincloth project, that's for sure. A company or a market can tell immediatly whether a message is nothing but a p.r. stunt or if it comes from the heart and is therefore authentic. If it's not authentic, it will be dismissed.

We're at the mercy of control freaks

We live in a time in which control and regulation are increasingly regarded as essential. Regulation originating from legislation like the Sarbanes-Oxley Act, with all its mandates and requirements for financial reporting, requires hundreds of millions in investments in systems and organizations whose job it is to make sure firms are following all the rules. These days, accountants are making so much money as a result of these excessive controls that they hardly know how to spend it all. I know of one large European bank that actually boasts that one of every ten of its employees is charged with exercising internal control over the others. Bravo!

Ten thousand employees from all kind of large organisations sit through ethics courses. Which they detest, by the way. And every day directors of large organizations are increasingly worried that they will be the next to fail and be indicted. Anxiety rules! That spells death for innovation and entrepreneurship.

It's hardly surprising that genuine entrepreneurs are getting quickly out of the stock market one after the other. Quarterly orientation and the climate of anxiety resulting from all sorts of legislation based on mistrust attack the entrepreneurial and creative spirit of organizations until finally there is no alternative but to return to long-term planning and as a result the interest of the organisation.

Am I saying that Sarbanes-Oxley, with its rules and regulations, spells the end of entrepreneurial America? Certainly not, because transparency is of vital importance. But the push for an all-pervasive system of control has become so strong, particularly with respect to companies whose stock is publicly traded, that the fertile ground for entrepreneurship and creativity is being lost.

Watch out for the liar

Authentic leadership and transparancy are, after all, very closely related. Authentic leaders are transparent. If they weren't, members of the organisation would quickly realize that they were dealing, not with a genuine human being, but with an actor or a liar. Or leaders who regard themselves as indispensable, because power has gone to their head. A leader who's started to believe in the reality of the play in which he has a leading part. Such leaders have lost their authenticity. As a result, they no longer feel bound by petty rules and regulations. That was at the root of one of the Enron problems. Authenticity was lacking and, with it, went transparancy. Caution is thrown to the wind, opening the way for a flood of inproper actions.

The central question for any large organisation should be whether you want to be a ruler or a leader. Do you work on a basis of trust or of distrust? It's abundantly clear that most organizations these days operate on the basis of distrust. It's a lousy system.

The atmosphere that prevails in an organization founded on a bedrock of ever-increasing regulations, anxiety, control, and suspicion, is not one in which creativity, innovation, entrepreneurship, and inspiration can hope to flourish. On the contrary. Slowly but surely, such organizations will go under. They will take with them all the cocksure assumptions that they found so satisfying. But who found them so satisfying? Not the employees of the organization. Nor the customers. For those two groups the need will be fundamentally different.

Where does this distrust come from?
Organizations and the people who work for them get their energy from things that inspire them. This could be leaders who have the power to inspire, or tasks that inspire and provide a challenge. Or it might be the stimulating work environment that one shares with colleagues. Satisfied customers or positive press coverage of an ambitious organization can inspire. But seldom will people be inpired by anxiety managers, excessive regulations, or distrust. Trust, on the other hand, does inspire. When an organisation fundamentally distrusts its employees and, as a result, loads them down with all kind of rules, while at the same time announcing that it wants to create room for innovation and creativity, it's hard to see this as anything but a joke. It's patently dishonest. Not genuine and thus a fraud.

"Creatively undertaking" and "thrillingly inspiring" are phrases that sound nice. Because they have positive connotations. Most People feel good when they hear them.

And if you think about the word "thrilling" and then look at the concerted effort to impose all kinds of rules, you see the painful difference. The more closely you look at what's going on, the more clearly you realize that we are murdering the thril. Organizations that are thrillingly creative and as a result inspire employees and customers, are fairly scarce. Scarce, if you weigh the full meaning of the words "inspire" and "thrilling." Because certainly some organizations exist where it's a pleasure to work.

I have often wondered where those lists of "the best companies to work for" come from. Because more often than not those lists include companies you wouldn't want to be caught dead working for. Do they really ask the right questions when they compile those lists?

Leaders in love with their image but blind to their organizations

Do leaders of large companies see the need for creative entrepreneurship and for inspiring their employees, thrillingly or otherwise? Yes, of course, if they are authentic leaders. But the self-deceivers, the chief executives who strut through the world convinced of their own importance, have long since lost their ability to look at their organization. Their ability to see. And from such leaders you can hardly expect the ability to perceive the long-term importance of creativity.

I truly believe that from time to time a wink of blue shows through the overcast sky of regulation and control. But it lasts only an instant — just long enough to provide hope that there's more blue out there. No one would argue that creativity and inspiration are to be found solely among managers. They are present throughout the entire organization. But leaders will have to give their full support to the creative and entrepreneurial shaping of their organization. Otherwise, every initiative will die a silent death.

If loincloth projects are initiated for the sole purpose of stimulating entrepreneurship, innovation, and creativity, the deception will be quickly noted throughout the organization. Because with the very first quarterly report that doesn't meet expectations, intervention will quickly follow.

Only with the full and genuine backing of its leaders can an organization be made truly creatively entrepreneurial and thrillingly inspiring. Without that support, every effort will fail. But with that support, a truly incredible amount of energy can be generated in all layers of the organization, the kind of energy that can move mountains.

From glum to fun

One day, I had to give a speech to about fifty managers. The occasion? I had just been appointed general director. After the chairman of the board introduced me, he turned the podium over to me. With no preparation, I was supposed to give a speech. I took a minute to think of what I should say and then decided just to say what I sensed, what I felt. And what I sensed was that those fifty managers sitting out there were really not very happy. They were a sad bunch. Glum. They weren't laughing. They had more or less given up. At least that's how it felt.

By talking openly, I seemed to have opened a valve: You could sense a big sigh of relief. I went on talking for about half an hour about things that had to do with enjoying your work, even having fun. Applause and a visibly happier group. I sat down next to the chairman, who complimented me on my speech, but added, "Better not talk too much about having fun, because that's not good for the bottom line."

Not good for the bottom line! In all my experience, I never once found that cheerful, motivated, creative, and inspired employees failed to boost productivity and, with it, the bottom line. Is the problem that having a good time, or having fun, will often be associated with partying and boozing and wasteful spending? Is that what's at work here? The truth is that inspiring employees and customers generates energy, with which you can do all kinds of things.

Creative entrepreneureship and thrillingly inspiring leadership can give organizations a human face again, can provide a counterbalance to the kind of distrust that has become the rule. Balance must be restored. Because by going overboard with rule-making, many organizations threaten to lose their balance. Or they unfortunately lost it a long time ago.

The reluctant return of the entrepreneur

The need for a return to fundamental ideas like creativity, entrepreneurship, thrilling and inspiration is being recognized, if only gradually. Leaders of a number of large companies have become aware that cost-cutting and controlling have been taken to the limit. They are looking for growth, new markets, which means creativity. But creating or generating energy after suppressing it for so long, or allowing it to emerge only sporadically, isn't that easy. And the call for creativity and innovation, coming after a period when all kinds of budgets have been slashed, may not be readily understood. Or trusted.

Someone told me once that there are two ways organizations can increase their profits. One is by lowering the costs, the other is to increase turnover (and to keep the cost down as a result). The first method will be handled by the managers, the second by the entrepreneurs. What's interesting here is that the entrepreneur looks for the solution in the market, while the manager often first looks internally.

And this brings us to a crucial point. We must realize that the only way to succeed in making an organization creatively entrepreneurial and thrillingly inspiring is by working together with the outside world. With the market, and with the customers. Look at the ever tempting offers of courses you can take on the internet. All sorts of ways of working from within the organization to improve its market performance. But seldom or never ways of bringing views from the outside world that might improve the organization.

The impetus to become creative and entrepreneurial can only come from the market, from the customer. From working together with the customer. And that is difficult and often quite scary. Further, inspiring customers or letting them become inspired can only take place through having contact with that customer. And this, too, is difficult and often scary. But very rewarding.

The goal of this book Rip off Your Necktie and Dance is to make a contribution toward helping corporations become creatively entrepreneurial and thrillingly inspirational. I realize that the word "do" plays a crucial role in this process. The best means of getting my message across, it seems to me, is to share experiences and tell stories about how this makeover can be achieved, and how to translate words into action. Into deeds, into doing.

But before one can get around to doing, a few fundamental obstacles have to be confronted. One has to determine what needs to be done. And what needs to be done is for someone to get up and take the power away from the control freaks. When will the real entrepreneurs seize the reins, take control? Clear the way for the original thinkers!

During the writing of this book, I was struck by the meteoric rise of the influential American trendspotter Marian Salzman. She got a lot of publicity with her definition of The New Man, the 'metrosexual'. Men are becoming male, she said. And that is, of course, is an interesting point of view to keep in mind when we look for true leaders, although these can be women as well as men. The metrosexual, according to Salzman, can talk about culture, is an ideal father for the kids, can talk about sports with other men, and can talk about feelings with women. She calls soccer star David Beckham the "epitomy of metrosexuality."

We're talking about a new kind of man here, and the time calls for a new kind of leader — one who can walk into a corporation and say, Rip off your necktie and dance!

Creative

creative

Narrow Minds & Rigid Strategies

One of our customers is a supplier of parts to the automobile industry. Everything looked good. Not a cloud in the sky. So the message we got from the director came as a shock: "If we continue on our present course, with business steadily improving, in a few years we won't exist." You could imagine the scenario: a few thousand employees in posts throughout the world would lose their jobs. And a number of unique manufacturing techniques, fine-tuned over the years, would also be lost.

What was the matter? First of all, there was the recession in the automobile industry. As a result, the car maker was putting more and more pressure on the supplier to produce parts more efficiently and to bring down the cost. Another factor: production of parts was being moved to countries in Eastern Europe and Asia, where labor was cheaper and where this supplier did not have any factories. In these emerging markets there were strong competitors who offered high quality at competitive prices. Finally, the car manufacturers had also acquired large sections of the production process (insourcing): they were manufacturing most of the parts themselves. The only parts they bought were those that did not fit into their own production plans or demanded special techniques. Thus, the supplier was in a commodity bind, without many possibilities to provide what others could not, and was suffering from constant pressure to lower the cost.

This situation did not arise overnight. Throughout the previous ten years, management had pressed for production improvement, specialization, and cost control. In fact, a factory came on line that delivered technically high-end products, but by the time the factory opened, Asian competitors were already catching up. Besides which, the company had devoted all its energy to a single market — the automotive sector. Meanwhile, existing markets and customers from other sectors, including the construction industry, were downsizing in order to achieve greater efficiency and focus. As a result of narrow thinking and rigid strategies, the company had dug its own grave.

creative

Where is the breakthrough?

The chairman of the board had a good grasp of the problem the company faced. He knew that diversity, innovation, and production development were needed to make the company less dependent on one sector. The question was: How to achieve that goal? The company had consistently discouraged initiative, creativity, and radical change. How could you bring this back? And, preferably, bring it back fast?

Working closely with him, we came up with a way to tackle the problem that would quickly achieve results. Our starting point was the power of the people in the company. Even though creativity and possibilities for renewal had been discouraged, they had not disappeared. We had to find ways to awaken those abilities and to encourage employees to use them for nothing less than the survival of their own company.

Learning to Think Ahead

To reach that result, I regularly use the strategy of the Nightmare Competitor. And I did so in this case. We organized a top conference of the complete management force of the company, including the holding company and subsidiaries, with the goal of moving us into two worlds:

1. A world in which a great opportunity exists that can guarantee the survival of the company. For example: a large car manufacturer is compelled to come up with a single particularly popular car model and select a supplier who will be responsible for all replacement parts during the next fifteen years.
2. The second scenario envisions a situation in which a small group of technicians has more than once come up with an innovative plan that has been rejected by top management. After years of frustration, they start up their own company or sell the technology to the competitor.

During the conference, the managers received detailed reports concerning the market situation, the economy, the automobile industry, and so on, which enabled them to get a firm understanding of it. On the basis of this information, we drafted two editions of the in-house magazine, both of them dated 2011, in which the scenarios came alive in interviews and background articles. The managers, devided in groups, were asked to come up with concrete answers for both scenarios: How would the company catch a golden opportunity like the fifteen-year spare-part contract? What kind of innovation plans could that small group of frustrated managers have come up with if it had been allowed to proceed instead of being stifled? Which innovative ideas were ignored or deep-sixed?

In the beginning, it felt strange. Which is only to be expected if your creativity has been suppressed or stifled for so long. But after a while the energy came back. Often, new ideas came from people you would otherwise never have heard from. Some managers didn't dare put their thoughts on the table without first asking permission from their superiors. One asked if he really had to cooperate on a doom-scenario involving his own employer, being slow to understand that the result could decide the future of his employer. But, by the hour, the energy increased. As if until now it had been frozen and was suddenly starting to thaw. One manager shouted out that he finally felt that he was master of his own destiny. The directors of one large division set themselves the goal of generating 20 percent of sales from new products or new markets.

There were moving testimonies as employees opened up. Some told of how long they had been worried about the company. Others said that different strategies had never before been discussed as openly as now. The company developed an energy flow that allowed it to create its own future. That flow did not originate from nuts-and-bolts analyses and hard facts. Fantasy (the scenarios), imagination (artwork, the special-edition magazines), and personal contact were indispensable ingredients.

creative

CREATIVITY – HAVING A BALL!

To make something that does not exist — is that creativity? Or the talent to be able to make something? A creation is a bringing to life, and creativity is the ability to create. What's hard for one person is easy for the next. During my student days I admired a friend who was majoring in mathematics. Math was a subject I had difficulties with; for him it was very easy. I envied his ability, but he said that, for him, doing math was a piece of cake. It was the other way around when it came to languages, which he had a very hard time with. I then realized that difficulty is a relative concept.

Michelangelo said once that, for him, sculpting was nothing more than freeing the scupture from the marble enclosing it. The sculpture already existed; it just had to be freed. Writers often have the story already in their head. They only have to write it down. So does that mean that creativity comes easy for some people? Does everyone have it, but with most people it just doesn't come out?

Never before

Several years ago I was in charge of a company in the San Francisco area. It produced virtual images for films and TV. These days that technology is in common use and few films are made without some special effects produced with computer technology. Back then, however, it was cutting edge, spectacular, visionary.

The founder of the company was an original thinker. And they are a rare species. Because I am convinced that there are very few people who can think outside the box — who can come up with something that's truly original. Original thinking means to think up something that has never been done before. It is also creativity, but in my eyes with a higher standard. To come up with an idea that is totally new, does that exist? Well, we will never know for sure, because there's always the chance that, at some time somewhere else in the world, someone came up with a similar brilliant idea. But let's assume for the moment that an original thought — a thought or concept that seems to come out of nowhere — doesn't occur very often. Most forms of creativity are based on uniting, modifying or — to view it from another perspective — manipulating existing ideas.

Can you visualize it?

This original thinker had the most bizarre ideas and thoughts — day in and day out. The art lay in choosing those things you could do something with. But the more original the ideas, the harder it was to filter out the viable ones. Why? Because a really original thought is rarely recognized. It's just too absurd to get your head around.

creative

During the French Revolution, it never occurred to the revolutionaries that, before they stormed the barricades, they should discuss strategy with each other on their cell phones. The concept of a telephone didn't exist and couldn't even be thought of. To think up something that does not exist, for which there is no demand (but a need for it!) and which nobody can imagine — the whole thought is ridiculous.

I think that this is the purest and highest form of creativity. But never or rarely appreciated. There was no need to create virtual images that looked real in a film or on television twenty-five years ago), and therefore there was no market. Now there is no visual market without virtual images. Discovering something for which there is no demand, but for which there is a need, is very difficult.

Take the very first word processing program for the PC. Until it came into being, the PC was just a sort of refined calculator. It was only after word processing was conceived that the PC explosion took place. One calls something like that a "killer-app". Afterward, everyone says that the word processing program wasn't revolutionary because it was just a logical next step. But the person came up with the idea was an original thinker. Back in the early days when IBM said that five large computers would suffice to meet the world's needs, there was no demand for hundreds of millions of PCs with which people could communicate with each other. Bill Gates, who was not even born at that time, had as his dream that everyone would have a PC (or something like it). IBM missed its chance. There was a tremendous need in the market for a product that would enable people to communicate more efficiently with each other. But the PC was not viewed as the means that could meet that need. That was simply inconceivable. In short, there was clearly a great need here and no demand..

Thinking of something that doesn't exist yet
Try that at a large efficiently organized company. You go to your boss and ask if he'll let you work on the development of a product for which there is presently no demand. If he looks surprised, you might add that there is a need for it, but no demand. Therefore no market. You want to come up with an idea that does not exist. The market has no clue about it and thus there is no demand for it. 3M came up with the Post-it. There was a need for it (as time would prove) but no demand. This way you can come up with thousands of ideas that have been thought up without a pre-existing demand. But a

latent demand, as they so nicely put it. My first business was in the field of artificial intelligence. Early on, during its first years, there was scarcely any demand. The market was clueless. It did not understand what artificial intelligence was, and did not know what to do with it. It required a tremendous amount of marketing. Talk, talk, and more talk. We called that "missionary marketing." Trying to be the first to sell something new to the market. Until you reach a critical mass and have acquired enough examples to make your case. Then a demand starts to come into existence. At least, if there is a need for the product. Missionary marketing is exponentially more difficult than ordinary marketing. But for my first company the biggest obstacle to attracting capital was that there was no market for the product and therefore no demand. Because bankers usually look for a proven market, a market based on solid numbers. But an entrepreneur senses the need…and creates the demand. And a manager sees the need and supplies the demand.

Something everyone does every day

Everyone has creative abilities. Within companies and large organizations there usually is no call for those abilities. So most people do not exhibit them. We are talking here about creativity in the larger sense — the combining of existing things and putting them to different uses; the creating of something new from something that already exists. So something that everyone does every day. And that we learned to do as a child. Drawing, singing, playing, and all kinds of things that children do all day long. And they enjoy doing them. But over the years that behavior has been channeled into tidy little rows, like obedient school children.

Do what your boss tells you to do. Be on time at your work. Sit down in that office. Go home late. Do not do this or that because someone else does it already. Don't think if you have not been asked to think. All kind of slogans that have become the norm at many large organizations. Why do we speak of "the first hundred days" when a new manager starts at a company? Because they have not yet been contaminated by some rigid set of rules and thus are still able to think of something new. In time, everyone will settle into the established routine of thinking and doing, and it will become increasingly difficult to be creative. Certainly if creativity is not actively encouraged. Because creativity creates chaos, it costs money, and because there is no demand for it. Just think of what kind of restrictions we impose on ourselves by curbing that creativity! Thousands of possibilities to increase sales — and thus boost profits — are passed up. Simply because we find it too scary to let the creativity run free.

creative

Open the windows

The main reason organizations operate this way is because it is too scary to become really creative. All sorts of phony excuses are made up to avoid being creative. The main one is: It only costs money and never gives any results. This happens even at companies that were launched on the basis of a creative idea. When the Dutch company Philips decided to produce its first light bulb, there was a need but hardly any demand. There were no sockets to screw in the light bulbs. But the creative Philips saw and felt the need and quickly set about creating the demand. That was pure entrepreneurship. Undoubtedly in those times there were several much larger organizations that probably could have made much better light bulbs. But they did not see the demand, and did not think that there was a market for such a thing. Which, at the time, in fact was true.

Skype is a logical reaction to the wish to be able to phone cheaply and the existence of the internet. In 1996 thousands of people saw this coming. At that time, software appeared on the market with which you could phone each other cheaply via the internet. It was all still very primitive and of poor quality. But it was available. How is it possible then that it was only in 2005 that Skype finally became a phenomenal success and was sold to eBay for millions of dollars? And that the president of the American telecomfederation agrees that Skype may change the telecom world forever?

Destroyed by a newcomer

It is really mystifying that a phenomenon that everyone a decade ago saw coming was not acknowledged by the establishment. It is curious that the establishment allowed its market to be wiped out by a newcomer. I admit that it is, of course, the result of a combination of a desire to prevent cannibalism and reduction in price. But I am convinced that distrust of creativity played a decisive role. Because nothing would have been easier than to free up a group of entrepreneurial and creative spirits inside an established telecom company and give them a chance to create that so-called "nightmare competitor."

Creativity is the most important weapon in the survival of any organization. To put things in order, to manage, to steer, to calculate — we can do that. All this is clearly overseeable and it can be talked through (and if things go according to plan) it will be under control. But the art of creating, and the environment in which creative ability is valued, is of vital importance for every organization. An environment in which one is allowed to create, in which one is allowed to be able to be creative, is necessary for every large organization. I am talking on purpose about large organizations, because smaller companies and organizations tend to encourage and stimulate creativity naturally. Because the smaller companies are often closer to the market, their employees respond more quickly. And creativity is more easily stimulated.

Use the creative juices

At larger organizations there is frequently a kind of unwritten code of acceptable behavior. Even though it has not been formulated by the management. It is of vital importance that management stimulates and displays creative behavior. Otherwise the stimulus for creative behavior will soon disappear. Activities that depart from the hard-and-fast rules or traditions of how things have always been done must be allowed, encouraged. One should not squash innovation.

And does that entail risks? Yes, because all kinds of things can go wrong. But don't worry. You can manage the process of creativity easily. You can keep the risks under control. But the most important thing is that the vital essence of every company must never be lost — the enormous resource of its creative ability. Because every person has it. You only have to activate it.

Creativity manifests itself in many different ways, but everyone is creative. Some will come up with something that others had never thought about. Others will see opportunities to improve work processes by degrees, gradually. Yet others will see the advantages of applying new technology.

It is particularly important to appreciate all creativity and to put the right kind of creativity in the right place. That is how an original thinker should develop market-oriented initiatives, not by micromanaging the innovation of critical processes. A good leader appreciates the creative people in his organization and takes care that each one is provided a place where his or her creativity can blossom.

creative

You want to *play*

One of the most important research centers in the world is the Xerox Corporation's Palo Alto Research Center (Xerox PARC). For many years all kinds of ideas have emerged from the center. Everyone knows the Microsoft Windows Operating system. It was incubated, you might say, in the Xerox PARC think tank. A fantastic place where you can play freely. There are very few places like it in the world. Maybe the Bell Laboratories, or the Bell Labs of the former AT&T, was such a place. Maybe they still are, even though I have the impression that these days they do much more applied research. The element of play has slipped into the background.

What you hear about these places is that all kinds of astonishing discoveries are hatched in them, which then rarely come to fruition. You also hear complaints that Xerox itself never did anything with the Windows Operating system.

I'm just playing with the thought…

One of the most stimulating figures at Xerox PARC was Chief Scientist John Seely Brown. He was the brains of the laboratory. I met him once at a conference we had organized for the board of trustees of a large multinational company. The conference was held in The Idea Factory in San Francisco. John Seely Brown was able to make the board of trustees actually play with their thoughts. He brought to the table ideas that had never occurred to anyone before. In short, they were completely original. Later, I met him again and I always considered him one of the prime examples of "playing." John Seely Brown said — and it's something leaders should remember: "The job of leadership today is not just to make money. It's to make meaning."

John Seely Brown and John Kao were friends. And John Kao played an important part in my life. Kao is a Chinese-American; his parents were professors in China. After World War II his parents fled to the United States. A son was born there. What would become of him? Maybe he would be a professor, as well. But John chose to be a musician and was an accomplished jazz pianist. He made it as far as keyboard artist in a number of different well-known bands, one of which was Frank Zappa's. But finally his genes kicked in and he became a professor at Harvard University. One of the nation's top universities. He chose a field of study that nobody else was interested in: Innovation Management. When a dean asked him how he planned to apply his studies in practice, John's reaction was: "Nobody has ever written about that." Exactly!

creative

John Kao worked for fourteen years at Harvard on the development of Innovation Management. During this time he also wrote his bestselling Jamming: The Art & Discipline of Business Creativity. But after fourteen years he had had enough — enough students, enough lessons. John quit, packed up, and took off for San Francisco, the place to be in the Nineties if you were interested in creativity and playing.

John wanted to play again! And not only at the piano, jamming with a band. He wanted to play with ideas and companies. He arrived in San Francisco and rented a vacant factory, previously a sweatshop in which Chinese women sewed clothes. The amazing thing is that he had no idea what he was going to do in that factory. He took a chair and sat down in the empty space to think. Let it happen. He placed a large Steinway in the center and started to jam. Because that is his way. Slowly, all kinds of talented people joined him and the factory became a place where companies could come and jam. Musicians had been doing this for decades, centuries — getting together and improvising on a theme. Playing as if they had been together in a band for many years. The best kind of playing. In a flow, together, enjoying.

Getting away from the world for a moment

John Kao was creating there, in San Francisco, in what he called The Idea Factory. A factory where companies could create and fine-tune their ideas while playing. That is where I learned how important a play environment is. It's impossible to play in a dull office space. You play in a sandbox or in a playground. In The Idea Factory, John played the piano and inspired people. I arrived there in 1999, with a group of customers. We had a session there that I will never forget. It seemed to me that I just disappeared for a moment from the world. When we were standing outside again, one of my customers said, "Leen, I get the feeling that now you're going to do something different." And that was true. At that moment I decided that being the CEO of a large company was not for me. I wanted to play more than was permissible in the world that surrounds a CEO. From that moment on a friendship developed slowly between John and me, which finally ended up in the two of us starting an Idea Factory in Europe. An environment in which by now hundreds of companies have had creative sessions. The place is very important. It's not everywhere that you can let your thoughts flow freely. And not everywhere can you play with each others' thoughts. The atmosphere, the location, is crucial. And from 2000 on all kinds of people started to play in the Idea Factory.

After a few years of playing, we learned that playing a little closer to the companies also paid off. To play inside a company is hardly possible, and is usually unacceptable. But one can play just outside. And people will notice and be enormously stimulated.

Playing hard

Playing is not allowed — we had to unlearn that. At the end of the Nineties and the beginning of 2000 it looked like companies were becoming more accepting of a play culture from within. Several books on the subject appeared. But with the explosion of the internet, acceptance disappeared. Financial control was the new order of the day. Playing was nonsense and anyway it didn't pay off. Even so, the annual reports of several companies will claim on their web sites that they have "high standards and values and make a contribution to human development," or words to that effect. It's often just the usual marketing lingo — all talk and no action. Though the employees would very much like to see their company contribute to human development.

Because when children play, they share. They improvise, compete, meditate, put their heads together. They behave in all kinds of ways that we as adults also know a lot about. (The Play Ethic by Pat Kane). The kinds of behavior we should encourage in our company's environment as well.

Take a look at the following three websites: www.idiotideas.com, www.idiotsidea.com and www.idiotbrain.com. People smile when they see the names, which help to stimulate the most idiotic ideas. Because, after all, what is idiotic? Is it something brilliant, or something which nobody ever thought of? And, for that very reason, valuable. To play with ideas is what John Kao is doing. To play with ideas is what happens on these websites. Playing with ideas is what all of us should do much more often. But how many organizations have truly tried to make room for play, playing, playing around?

At Google, playing is obligatory. All employees are given the opportunity to spend 20 percent on company time doing things they enjoy doing. Fun things. Seen from the outside, it produces a playful company culture. People feel that they are allowed to do whatever they wish. But it turns out that Google derives its innovation strength precisely from that 20 percent of play time. Almost all market introductions from Google, from Gmail to Google Earth, turn out to be rooted in play projects of individual employees.

It's got to stay fun

As mentioned, in their mission statements all companies talk about how they treat their employees — the pleasant or stimulating workplace atmosphere and all the rest of it. But mostly it's all just empty talk. Or the pleasant work atmosphere is the first thing to go when the economy goes into a slump. Seriously, which companies in the The West are fun to work in? Which companies leave room for creative talent to play, to explore? Many companies consider themselves loose and creative, but when it comes down to it, they fire their most vital people as soon as the market experiences a downturn. Loyalty and the long-term view are almost nonexistent. Obsession with quarterly reports leads to short-term thinking and leaves little room for creative behavior.

Do something crazy

All studies that look into the future indicate that in the coming years the war for talent will escalate dramatically. There will be a great shortage of employees with the required technological skills. While presently we make it hard for foreigners to enter the country, in future years we will be flying them in on deluxe Boeings. Because we will need them.

A corporate environment in which one is allowed to play appeals to normal human needs. There is nothing strange about that. What's strange is that most companies don't do anything about it. Employees are not fooled by companies that say they're going to do something and then don't follow through. This sort of thing just turns them against the organization.

Loosen up. Let yourself go. Do something crazy. Behave like a child from time to time. Shall we start to play?

How about doing nothing for a change?

Do nothing. Do absolutely nothing. A horrifying thought for vast populations of God-fearing managers. Managers who feel that everyone must work very hard. That you really should be sitting in the office at eight o'clock in the morning, even though you've been stuck in traffic jams for hours. So you leave home earlier. "Yes, I really do work eighty hours a week." What a sad flock of sheep…

Trainees with a large oil company apparently pull their shirts out of their pants by the end of the afternoon, roll up their sleeves, and, above all stay longer at their desks than the boss. Walk up and down the corridors looking as if they are really going all out for the boss. That there is no limit to their dedication to the job. Apparently, that's what's expected of them. Otherwise, no normal person would ever behave like a gang of lunatics. But the pressure to become a workaholic must come from somewhere.

I recently joined a small golf tournament in California that was a lot of fun. Delightful. With pleasant people at an exceptional location. Even so, the day before the start a CEO called to say that he was too busy to come. Of course, something can always come up, but in this case I got the strong impression that this CEO felt that he was indispensable. A lot of people think that way. Even though the company will surely function quite smoothly if one fine day they don't show up at the office. Rationally, they are aware of this. But they are worried — anxious that maybe someone will take over if they don't show how hard they are working. At all times.

creative

All those anxieties. All kinds of situations that people create in their own minds. Because they're not real. So, let the other guy take over. Let the company miss you. Because doing nothing, instead of getting caught up in a workaholic frenzy, is enormously productive. And this, this is something that is very hard to make people believe.

Empty-headed

When are you creative? When are you able to find solutions to difficult problems? When are you most creative? Well, when your head is empty. When you are not pressured by time. Ask someone who is creative to create something really fast. Preferably now. Ask someone in advertising to come up with a great idea on the spot. Usually they won't be able to. Good ideas arise, originate spontaneously in your head. Solutions to difficult problems occur when you're taking a shower, or shaving, or walking the dog. We all know this, but still we don't give ourselves the space to come up with new ideas. Because we have to work. Few people realize how they are spending their time. As a result, they let invaluable time slip through their fingers like fine sand. Time flies like an arrow. One moment it's there, the next minute it's gone, disappeared. Just doing nothing is a terrifying thought for many. Because so much has to be done…

And nothing has to be done! Certainly not if it takes away time from things that really require your attention, that really matter in life. Like your children, your partner, your self, your friends, the world, your employees — and I could go on. All kind of things that are more important than your work. But it's much easier to escape in your work, pretending that that is of more importance than anything else.

What keeps us occupied?

About once a month I go with a group of managers to a castle in France. We don't hurry. Don't get up too early, don't rush, stop along the way. After we arrive at the place, a medieval castle, we first have lunch, with a good glass of wine. After lunch we give ourselves time to recuperate. Then, by which time it's at least four o'clock, we have a discussion while sitting in front of a huge medieval fireplace with a roaring fire. The kind of fireplace in which you have to throw tree trunks and where the flames rise about six feet high. And what do we discuss? Ourselves and each other. Things that really concern us. Causes that inspire us, move us, fascinate us. Stories that can bring tears to your eyes. Telling each other stories that are genuine, that come from the heart. We listen. A lot of listening. To each other, but sometimes also to yourself. At our ease, staring into the fire. Contemplating what is being said. You get into a flow that way. You open up as a result and you share with others your most intimate thoughts. In trust. When do we ever do that? Well, almost never. Because nobody has time for that kind of thing.

The president of a bank was planning to attend one of these sessions in France. But he was another one of those who just could not resist canceling a week before we left. Too busy. Yes. Duty called. A few days of doing nothing obviously had the lowest priority on the calendar. Teach me how all those calendars work. Secretaries have been trained to plan everything down to the last minute. "No, sorry. Mr. X is booked solid for the next four months." Not a single open spot. Mr X could, of course, find an open spot! He has one — the open spot in his head. Are you crazy! If it's important you find an open spot immediately. If your child has an accident, don't you immediately find a spot? Then suddenly the calendar is no longer important. Yes, I can be quite emotional about this kind of thing. It is not that I didn't behave like this, for years. But these days I follow my own calendar. Because my time is valuable and I would rather not waste it on unimportant meetings, with people I do not really want to see. And I make sure that there are always plenty of empty spots.

To get back to the president of the bank for a moment, the one who had no time to come to France. First of all, I called him myself and told him that canceling was not allowed. That made some impression, but not enough. Then I sat down and wrote him a letter, (by hand, with a pen and a sheet of real paper!!) A cri de coeur, you might say. I asked him if he really thought that he was so important, that his presence at the bank was indispensable. And if he ever took the time to sit still, to do nothing, maybe for days on end, and then to contemplate what it all means to him. He joined us; his calendar had an open spot. So it was important after all, but difficult. I will never forget what he told me when we were at the airport in Toulouse waiting for our return flight. "Leen, it was unforgettable. I have grown…but it was too short. Much too short."

Better off

Of course, it was too short. We always take too little time for the things that really matter. We only take a moment to bring the children to school, we take a moment to say goodnight to them. We wave goodbye for a moment to our wives, we never go to the PTA evening at school, we have no time for friends. There's always too little time, because there are more important things to be done. Another guest in France cancelled, because suddenly a board meeting had been announced. When I told him that canceling was not allowed and that the company would be better off without him — a joke! — there was silence at the other end of the line. Better off without me, I could hear him think. Yes, and you are better off without that meeting, I would have loved to add. And then once again: "You are not allowed to cancel, because the balance of the group would be lost and I would have a problem." Hmm, yes, that would be a problem.

His reaction was: I'll be coming. Why do I always have to talk a blue streak to convince people that doing nothing is really good for them? Why do most of them join sort of surreptitiously? Do they say they're going to take a course or attend a seminar to make it sound better? Something like that. Imagine that you would have to tell your boss or your colleagues that you are going to do nothing for a few days. Do nothing? Are you crazy? We are so busy right now. You can't just leave and do nothing!
It goes without saying that those sessions in France are enormously productive. Following the afternoon session of doing nothing and talking with each other, in the evening we discuss those things that inspire people most. The sources from which people draw their strength and energy. You hear fantastic tales. Always totally authentic. Because if it is not authentic it will be worthless. You might as well work in that case.

We call those gatherings in France CORE sessions, because that is the goal: to penetrate to the core of things. To take the time to discuss and exchange ideas that really matter in life. With people who generally never do that kind of thing. Because they are too busy. The location is very important. And this place, this castle, dating back to the Middle Ages has positive energy. Some people are very susceptible to this. This place has been inhabited for thousands of years. First in the prehistoric age by cave dwellers, then the Romans. And even though the castle was destroyed in 1360, a very positive energy still rules. At some point I would like to understand how this is possible. Because the destruction could not have been pleasant. On the other hand, it is not for nothing that for thousands of years people have inhabited the place. They unconsciously looked for good places to live.

The right place
The message is: you have to carefully select the place where you let people do nothing. The location must provide them with energy. Energy to calm down. The peace and quiet needed to calm down. That's impossible at the office. Even though some can manage this. They just meditate an hour in the office every day. But that can only be done if it is your cup of tea. You have to learn to do that. But all those untrained people who want to do nothing — that has to be facilitated. There is still a long way to go before organizations encourage management to do nothing. Not all the time, but enough of the time. To enable

creative

them to be much more productive than they are at present. It will take some time before it is mandatory to do nothing from time to time. Before the organization realizes that this creates a better balance.

In the past it was a matter of pride to say that you were working eighty hours a week. That you just did not have a minute to spare. If somebody asked you "Are you busy?" you couldn't possibly reply that you have nothing to do. How can you be successful if you have nothing to do? We have to get over that. This whole business of being very busy. It's not good for us, certainly not in connection with our work. And not at all if it ends up in compulsive behavior.

Is that allowed?
A well-known CEO of a large American concern works so hard that he is rarely at home. Flies all over the world. Starts every morning at seven. Is hardly ever at home in the evening. Often sleeps in hotels. Do you recognize this? And to make matters worse, he expects this terrible behavior from his colleagues. That he drives himself like this is one thing. To require it of others, to turn it into a corporate culture is very troubling.

At a speech I gave to some 300 managers at a company of which I was the director, I remarked that it was half past six and that I really had to go home now because I had promised to be with the children that evening. I felt that I was already too late, and I didn't think much about that remark. But I got a lot of questions and emails about it. They all asked the same question: whether that was allowed at the company. Whether one was allowed to have such a priority. The question was really surprising to me, because I hadn't noticed yet that this was part of the corporate culture at the company. To work hard and keep on going until late in the evening.

If I do not work in the evening I am still a little restless. Sometimes when I read a book sitting in front of the fireplace I even feel guilty. These are both withdrawal symptoms that come from kicking the addiction. I once heard that smokers experience the same feeling of discomfort when they have just stopped smoking. To do nothing, to think that one is not busy is difficult. And it is often not appreciated. But doing nothing from time to time is the best remedy against stress. The best way of solving problems. Is the way of staying happy and becoming truly yourself.

To do nothing should be a mandatory part of work. Maybe you will become very busy with doing nothing.

creative

The beauty of flow

creative

Sometimes it feels as if everything goes by itself. As if you're in a trance. You never get tired. You could go on forever. A wave of happiness comes over you in which you can accomplish far more than normally. Working long hours isn't a matter of heart slogging or pushing yourself to an extreme, but happens in an energy high. As if you're on drugs (and maybe your body is actually tapping into some natural energy source).

Not long ago the Spanish Villareal soccer club was playing in the semifinals of the Champions League 2006. Quite an accomplishment because before that nobody gave the club a chance. But suddenly the team enjoyed a run of success. The players had wings on and the team played match after match way beyond their ability. Everything went right. How had they gotten so far? What was the reason that the team could move mountains and that made the impossible possible? The answer was clear. They had come into a state of "flow". A constant stream of energy that lifted the players to a higher level, so they were almost floating. They were inspired by their goal (to get to the next round in the Champions League), and every time they reached that goal, the next goal was right in front of them — reaching yet another level. The victories they had under their belt gave them a sense of euphoria. Every victory was wildly celebrated. By the club, the fans, the newspapers, and, later, even by all of Spain. And the victories also acknowledged the possibility of reaching the title: "You see? It can really happen!" Unfortunately, the fairytale ended in a loss against the English team, Arsenal, and as a result the Spanish team could not play in the finals. But they did write history.

The strange thing is that when we speak about "flow". most people don't immediately think about their work. For many people, work is dull, a drag. A necessary evil. We do it for the money, or because we have to. Even though we spend roughly 40 hours per week at work. That's about a quarter of the total time and close to a third of the time we are active— i.e. when we are not sleeping. It is clear that not many people are able to apply the "flow" experience to their work. And calling up 'flow' or making it possible is not something companies can always do.

Turn on the flow

My first employer was a large multinational corporation. I was still young and I had a talk with the head of personnel of the division where I worked. "What is your ambition at our company?" he asked me. Well, I wouldn't mind reaching a management position, I said. He looked at me. "That is what everyone who comes here wants," he said. I had to be more specific. Then I mentioned that I wouldn't mind being the CEO. That was a new one to him. "You need at least thirty years of experience for a position like that," he said. "So I can't write this down." Real ambitions obviously were unusual. Or they weren't expressed out loud.

The experience with the personnel director was not the beginning of a flow experience, of course. Not very stimulating. How different these multinational companies would look if they were able to create flow for their employees. Imagine that every successful project, or every successful quarter, or every successful contact with a customer would feel like winning the next game in the play-offs for the Super Bowl! If that were to happen, the company would look completely different. It would inspire and fizz with creativity and previously untapped, unknown energy would be released. Fantasy? Utopia? The fact remains that flow exists, that it generates tremendous energy. And that for most people it hardly ever shows up at work.

On your toes

Shortly after my interview with the personnel director, I decided to start my own business. That seemed the best way to work out my ambitions. I would be immediately president of the company and my first goal would be instantly realized. I could immediately set myself new goals. In my own company I have had strong 'flow' experiences. I worked very hard but never had the feeling that it was a burden (there were times when people around to me thought differently about this, but that's another story). I could always find new goals that were inspiring, and every time the goals were confirmed with results and success. The company grew, became a success, and I later sold it.

It's generally thought that flow evolves from the right balance between challenge (inspiring goals) and skill (possibility of attaining one's object). A large challenge combined with little skill ends up in anxiety. Fear of failing. That does not create 'flow'. At one point I worked at a company that was rapidly expanding. At a certain point I decided that I needed another secretary, one with more skills and more work experience than the secretary who had been working for me. That's not a nice message to give anyone. When we started to talk about it, she turned out to be very relieved. She had felt pressured for many months and the accumulation of work-related pressure was stressing her out. She worked increasingly longer hours with increasingly less confidence in her skills, and increasingly fewer results. She had ended up in a state of cramped anxiety. You could say that it was a condition of 'anti-flow'. And she was glad that the moment had arrived in which she could get out of this situation, even though she might face new uncertainties.

It keeps on going

The other side of the coin is that few small-scale challenges combined with great skills spells boredom. That doesn't create flow either. Everybody knows the story of the businessman who takes early retirement at fifty-five. Accustomed to constant pressure, always in an adrenaline rush, his appointment schedule leaving no time for delays, always doing two things at once, he suddenly faces a void he has never encountered before. What should he do with all this free time, the lack of stimulus and incentive? At fifty-eight he has his first heart attack. He recuperates, but is never the same. At sixty-two he has become an old man, who is largely being looked after by his wife. When he is sixty-four, even before his official retirement age, he dies. And this also is a situation of "anti-flow", but of the opposite kind.

To achieve flow, our goals and our skills must be equally matched. The demands imposed on you to achieve your goals must lie within your capabilities. And as you work, those capabilities will increase — in other words, the skills. You are becoming more adroit, gaining experience and insight, etc. And as your skills increase, the goals may be (or must be) set higher. Flow demands increasingly complex goals. Flow never stands still. It is never static.

Along with a good balance between goals and skills, regular feedback is needed to attain 'flow'. If for years you have a goal in mind but never receive confirmation that you are getting closer to the goal, you lose the flow. I myself was in that situation, and I knew many people in my circle of friends and acquaintances who shared this feeling: the ones who always wanted to write a book. For years I had been planning to do so. Complete chapters were going through my mind day and night, but not a sentence was written down. Until the day you seriously start on it. Every chapter, even every page you write works like an affirmation of your dream, downshifting on the decision to really write that book. The book I had been thinking about for years, I wrote it in less than three months after all. And I don't want to romanticize this: sometimes it was easy and sometimes it gave me great difficulty. But clearly I found the flow of the work. And that is why it is written, and you are reading it now.

We're getting somewhere

That feedback can, by the way, consist of little things. Even small confirmations coming in from time to time can boost your energy. A sailor on the sea looks at water for days on end, but he gets his feedback from the progress on his navigation map. He "sees" the progress and gets courage from it. Other sailors get their feedback from dolphins that swim alongside, or icebergs which they narrowly avoid. It just depends why you are taking the trip, but confirmation that you are getting closer to achieving that goal is crucial to keep the flow going.

When recently we had to give a large presentation to a few big companies, we decided to scrap the power point presentation. Instead, we made a large poster, of about six feet across, on which the whole story was presented, with as little text as possible and mostly pictures. The result was tremendous. Instead of a sleepy public in the hall, we now had an active crowd, people who got involved in the project, surrounding the poster, pointing, gesturing, talking. Everyone could pro-actively point out the subject about which they were most enthusiastic and they got the concept immediately. In a jolt of energy, a lively discussion followed. Everyone wanted to take part in the proposed project. The poster turned out to be a devise that really stimulated the flow. It not only provided an overview of the whole proposal, but it also made it possible for everyone spontaneously and immediately to display their enthusiasm and energy, without having to wait until the end of the power point presentation after which they finally could voice their approval. The feedback time had been shortened considerably and the energy increased accordingly.

What's essential, then, is feedback and inspiring goals that are attainable. The goal comes first, of course, because the rest follows from it. In our projects we have many interviews with our customers and we ask them about their dreams and ambitions. Only personal dreams and ambitions count. There's no need to answer. And it is amazing to see how eager people are to talk. Personal dreams and ambitions are the motor behind the flow. The ultimate energy source. After all, it's all about personal happiness. Because personal happiness is precisely the essence of flow.

creative

Chaos and order

creative

You could compare an organization with a machine. The processes and the procedures are the cogs in a wheel. The suppliers deliver the components at the beginning of the production process, and at the end of the process the product will be moved out from the warehouses and the stores. Another point of comparison: the process can be regulated. Production can be speeded up or slowed down and, by making small changes in the production process, one can make small changes in the product. If more substantial changes are required, we can completely reconfigure the production process. But the production process remains central to the image of the machine. The organization as creator of order. Of regularity, predictability. Of total control.

Human resources

To many people this idea is not very attractive. People become "human resources", lumped together with a number of other resources which the organization consumes, like capital and raw materials. It also conjures up something dead and unchangeable. Where is the inspiration and the creativity in such a machine-like organization? And how is it possible for such an organization to flexibly react to a whimsical reality?

Besides which it seems that the organization machines that we have developed and are using are not always effective. All too often we hear of organization machines that grind to a halt or even derail. Think of stuffy bureaucratic organizations where certain things are simply "not done". Or of fraudulent excesses (especially when these come to our notice too late) that led to the total downfall of giants like Enron en Parmalat. Our lives are full of these things. And because organizations are important factors in the functioning of our society, the question is whether we want keep looking at it in a mechanical way.

The polar opposite of the machine could be total anarchy. The total absence of clear-cut rules. Everything is possible and everything is permissible. This in any case opens us up maximally to the outside world. You should be able to expect that any significant development in the market would inspire some individual to come up with a product and offer it to the market. Organizations might not be needed anymore, or they might arise spontaneously and disappear again. "Let a thousand flowers bloom," is sometimes said in company jargon. The organization as guardian of complete chaos. Of keeping open all possibilities.

Neither model works, of course. Imposing total order is ineffective, permitting complete chaos is inefficient. Total order leads to inertia by way of the limitations of the machine, and complete chaos leads to apathy because the lack of any directional logic and structure. Both lead to deathly passivity in which finally nothing happens anymore.

No alternative to blinders

There are plenty of examples of order-directed organizations that, because of a lack of flexibility, could not survive in their structure of that time. When the PC appeared on the horizon, IBM dismissed it as an irrelevant development of mainframe computers. Shortly after, the company suffered financially: it did not realize the importance of the PC in time. Existing rules and paradigms made that impossible. In the same way, the internet has put many publishers in a dilemma. The transition from the time of "knowledge is power" and profitable copyrights to free downloads and viral marketing strategies ruined a number of them. The computer giant and the publishers were both icons of the established order, and thought within the confines of the principle of manipulation, of protected, established interests, and procedures and rules that consolidated their power.

But there are just as many examples of chaotic conditions that did not turn out to be an alternative. There was the internet hype of the year 2000. Everything was possible, everything was permissible. One talked about a "New Economy" in which all the old paradigms were pushed aside. Sobriety and rationality were swept away. Common sense was left at home. That's how it seemed. One invested hundreds of dollars or Euros in a single internet subscriber, convinced that he would shortly make all his purchases via the web and that the provider could earn a percentage of the purchase price.

The stock market scandal story around World Online is engraved in the memory of many investors. When the share price tumbled, investors discovered that the founder had already sold her stake in the company, and when the WOL float collapsed shortly after, suspicion ran high. Inside knowledge and other irregularities were central to subsequent court proceedings, but the real cause, of course, was the absurdity of the market value itself.

This arrogant behavior was — as we all now know — mercilessly punished. And that also caused a lot of damage to "good" companies and initiatives. It came as a shock when AOL took over the old and trusted Time Warner in return for shares. The company value of Time Warner, which had been built up over decades, was in one fell swoop traded for — as became clear a few years later — marginal worth.

creative

Is there a balance somewhere?

That a balance between chaos and order must be maintained is self-evident. Chaos is required to preserve flexibility and creativity, order is essential to guaranteeing productivity and efficiency. But how do we maintain a healthy balance? How do we achieve the best possible balance?

Not so long ago we had to organize, in only a few weeks, a workshop for an important customer. That workshop was part of a larger program that we had come up with ourselves and in which only the outlines were firmly established. Everyone knew that the content of the workshop would set the direction for the whole program, but none of us knew exactly what the total program would be. In preliminary discussions, several attempts had been made to set up a plan that would include the long-time sequence of program events as well as the content of the workshop. But it seemed as if every time we nailed something down, something came loose elsewhere, and every possibility lay open again.

The search going on in our heads — and in the head of our customers, as well — was still so free-wheeling that nothing could be firmed up. It drove the project leader crazy. "Nobody here is making a decision!" he shouted in desperation. I tried to calm him down by telling that this was all part of a creative design process, but I understood his emotions: we had to satisfy an expectation and therefore concrete things had to be prepared, which required that final decisions had to be made. Until the last moment, everything stayed open. Then, only a few days before the start of the workshop, some kind of ordering flow developed. Suddenly all the loose ends fell in place and the end product materialized. And if you looked at the end result, it looked as if we had taken it from the associated companies. I have learned from this that it is not only a matter of achieving a balance between Chaos and Order. It is also timing: when is it time to let the ordering do its job of tidying up? I counted on the fact that in the heads of all those involved, the moment of pulling things into shape would announce itself without outside interference. Like a synchronization. And that is what happened.

Chaordic organizations

Recently I read a fascinating book written by Dee Hock. He wrote about the credit card situation in the sixties in the US. All banks were distributing cards and they guaranteed payment to the market. All the banks also extended credit to the cardholders and knew that, if it was not their own card, there would be a strong guarantee from another bank. The rules were clear. The machine worked. On paper at least. The result was that banks became focused on extending credit. After all, with every transaction they earned money. The business of collecting money via securities from other banks received much less priority. There was every assurance that they would get that money, eventually. The result was that the system became disorganized because the response time to weak credit lines and fraudulent transactions was delayed. The machine derailed.

Hock saw that the complexity of the credit system was too large to control in one organization model. That's why he chose the model of "self-organization". It worked like this. He created a cooperative in which the participating banks brought in their cards. All participating banks received an equal share in the cooperative. A charter was established, a code of conduct of goals and principles to which everyone would adhere. Besides which the cooperative was being divided in regions, each of which could freely develop its own processes, systems, and structures. Processes that were not local but that concerned everyone had to be referred back to the central committee for approval.

The cooperative took off, expanded exponentially. Today more than 22.000 competing banks are members, and every year they service a total of more than 750 million customers who generate more than a trillion transactions, for which the greatest degree of collaboration of all members is needed. In 1973 the cooperative received the world-famous brand name: VISA.

Hock called the way in which he brought this self-organization into existence — Chaordic Design — a contemporary organizing process that maintains the balance between Chaos and Order. One of my favorite examples of a chaordic structure is Wikipedia (www.wikipedia.com), the web encyclopedia on which thousands of people cooperate as volunteers, adding their knowledge to the related entries and in that way created a mega encyclopedia that by now, in volume and accuracy, has surpassed the Encyclopedia Brittanica. The goal (making knowledge accessible) and the principles (strict rules for contributors) of this chaordic design are so powerful that it has become a model of self-organization for schools in the dance between Chaos and Order.

creative

Nightmares
as a recipe

creative

All quiet on the front. Whenever the bulls are running and profits are high, it is usually pleasant to work in a company. Shareholders are happy, management and employees are proud, orders are coming in, and there are good vibes in the organization. In short, a happy existence. At least, that's how it seems. Because the better the market is, the more interest it gets from newcomers. The danger of competition is always lurking, and that is particularly true in a booming market with high margins.

At such times, a good market is vulnerable to the newcomer with the new idea. But there is another vulnerability. When things go so well with the market and the organization, there will hardly be any reason to do things differently. Why would you? And who would seriously start thinking about threats at a time when it seems that there are only opportunities. It is incredibly difficult to convince a company to ready its defenses against possible competition when all is going well. Before you know it, they call you paranoid. "But, sir," the doctor said to the patient, "the fact that you are paranoid does not mean that you aren't being followed." And that is the truth.

On the other hand, take for example a company like KPN, the Dutch national telecom company, which at the beginning of this millennium was struggling to survive. If a company lands in a similar situation and management is capable, it will often be ready to take drastic measures. And to act fast, because doing nothing means a death warrant. At that point, creating a sense of urgency is much easier than when a company is doing well in a healthy market. If things go badly, necessity is the mother of invention, as they say. But KPN was previously a monopoly, as all national telephone companies were. An unnatural situation in which

for a good
night's sleep

creative

competition was artificially suppressed. Under such circumstances, it is almost impossible to persuade a company to make changes. Competition is a blessing for any organization, even though it may not always feel that way. To my thinking, KPN functions a lot better now than it did before. Even though they have probably lost some market share, the customers are much better off than during the days of the state monopoly. And KPN has become more robust and innovative.

Who sees trouble coming?

Let's go back for a moment to the beginning. The company is running well, but the visionary management sees competition on the horizon or some threatening change in market circumstances. Quite a lot of companies and organizations see the barbarians appearing on the horizon in this global marketplace. So we are working on this for a company that supplies parts to the automobile industry and that is aware that the market is going to fundamentally change, with China going into production and with the relocation of production to Eastern Europe. Like the CEO told us: "Business is good, but if we don't do things differently instead of getting better all the time, we won't exist in a couple of years."

Companies that can foresee the threat on the horizon have to respond accordingly. By arming the company against the looming disaster. But how can you turn on the creative juices needed to confront the threat if everything is going so well? In such situations, we create a terrifying competitor. We call such a competitor who is a threat to the established order the Nightmare Competitor. A competitor so different, so vicious, and so dangerous that you get nightmares thinking about it.

As an employer, you can create Nightmare Competitor scenarios to wake up your company when it seems that everything's going smoothly, and to keep it on its toes by coming up with proactive strategies and alterations.

Winning the next war…

We first look at such a nightmare competitor "at random". Nightmare competitors often attack quiet, allocated markets, where a monopolist or an indolent oligopoly is making big profits thanks to good deals. But not only there. In our changing world, all markets are vulnerable to failure.

In 1995 Easyjet was established by the son of a millionaire Stelios Hajiloannou. In a short time Easy Jet conquered a large market share and became the terror of the established way of doing things. Why? Because Stelios consistently focused on providing the essential need of a large group of air passengers. Namely, to be able to fly reliably from A to B without any frills. By making this the uncompromising guideline for his business model, Stelios introduced to this market a whole new way of doing business, including a new price range.

Ryanair went a step farther. To some destinations flights are offered for free. How is that possible? By taking a good look at the 'source of money'. For whom is it important that many travelers arrive in B? Hotels, restaurants, vacation resorts, shops, and so on. Those interested parties sponsor the fares.

A Nightmare Competitor isn't just a new face on the horizon. No, he's someone who changes the rules of the game. And in such a way that nobody can ignore it. But, unfortunately, every long-established company is so stuck in its own culture, that it can't quickly copy the business model of the Nightmare Competitor.

There are many other examples, all of which illustrate the same point. Skype, for instance, has shown a tremendous success with the ability of telephoning via the internet. Years ago, Dell launched an attack on the establishment, by changing the logistics around PCs and giving the customer the possibility to configure his own PC. Dell these days is a market leader, but started out as a nightmare competitor that changed the rules of the game (logistical concept and customer self-service). We also know of course the immense impact of Amazon.com and Google. EBay emerged as a nightmare competitor with huge consequences. Because of eBay the business in dealing in secondhand goods was changed completely. If it used to be in former days a Business-to-Consumers model, with companies as intermediary between the selling party and the market, now it has become a Consumer-to-Consumer model. A completely different game with different rules and a different earnings style.

To attack or to defend?

So, they are nasty attackers, those Nightmare Competitors. Literally, your worst nightmare. They change the rules and you really have neither the time nor the possibility to respond adequately. Many things change, but one thing is for sure: they get you in your weaknesses or unutilized possibilities. The soft underbelly. St. George and the dragon and guess who is the dragon?

If you see them arrive in time, you could do something, one would think. But is that really the case? Ask an organization to create a strategy in an "easy" market. Does one come up with solutions which change the game? It is a well known fact that generals always fight the last war. Why

creative

was the Marginot Line built? Because the system had been designed by generals who had led troops in the World War I and that was a trench war. Oh yes, and the Netherlands and Belgium were neutral at that point and so the line didn't have to continue to the north. The nightmare we have seen: a blitzkrieg of tank divisions that went around the Maginot Line. That was a shock.

How can the generals be shaken awake and made to think seriously about the next war? My experience, and I have seen it happen in organizations that I led myself, but also with my present customers, is that the following works well.

Pound us into the ground

Start with the creation of a Nightmare Competitor. Let it be done by strategists, marketing personnel, and development managers from the organization, or, even better, by the high-potentials. That will give the necessary fresh look, but could also be well fitted into an MBA program. Of course, it will help to include a third party who will take care that it stays sharp. This will make a considerable difference in the accepted strategy of a company in good times. Because the assignment is: analyze the market, the trends and developments, the threats, your weak points, and then imagine that with unlimited resources you are allowed to set up a new company that competes with your own business on the market — what would that company look like? No interference from stockholders and therefore no restraints on your ability to change the rules. Go ahead, destroy us!

Once people are in the middle of the process, they will become enormously motivated and work with much pleasure on the Nightmare Competitor scenario. That should be no surprise, because this requires a strong demand on the combination of creativity, knowledge of the business environment, and professional skill. During a two-day summit for a large industrial company where New Business was the theme, we asked the top-management present to create a Nightmare Competitor like that, to generate a sense of urgency. A workshop with the management for each Business Unit followed after the Summit, to set up new business projects. In the preparation of the workshop of his business, the management director of one of the Business Units, very worried, asked if we were going to develop the Nightmare Competitor any further. That wasn't the intention, but the counter question was: is the projected competitor a serious threat? Because if so, the development of the scenario to sharpen the strategy is in every way worthwhile. Do not file it in a drawer as an amusing bit of playacting. Because you will regret this very much when that Nightmare Competitor emerges for real on the horizon.

What will we do with it?

What do we do once we have drawn up such a nightmare project? There are a few possibilities, depending on the situation. One option is to bring the Nightmare Competitor on the market under a different name. That can be done in one's own market, with behind it the idea that the new competitor will cannibalize the mother company, but probably will take away much more business from other competition. The Nightmare Competitor could also be launched in a different geographical market, where you yourself are not present yet, but other parties — including, perhaps, your local competition — are. This is an attacking variation. And, with luck, applicable within the home market.

Sometimes it's clear that, should the Nightmare Competitor enter the market, it would take away a lot of business and that even the taking away of business from the competitor would not be worth it. The fact that the Nightmare Competitor will appear at some point is practically inevitable. So what's to be done? Take care that all (especially the time-consuming) preparations have been taken to implement the model of the Nightmare Competitor oneself. Then, as soon as the nightmare appears, you'll be able to respond quickly and adequately. Until that time, you keep on profiting from the current business model. This is a defensive variant.

There is a third and also a defensive variant which speaks for itself. Analyze the threats of the Nightmare Competitor that you have developed and implement the right defensive measures from your existing business model. If they do not exist, or if you are not sure that they will be effective, then one of the other is a more prudent variant.

No matter what, by setting up the Nightmare Competitor as a realistic threat, a lot of strategic keenness is gained. It is an ideal strategy to apply in a situation in which the company is a monopoly or a market leader, or is succeeding in a stable profitable market. Don't fall asleep: the enemy is alert. This way you keep on creatively taking action, even in quiet times. And it is a big inspiration for participants — it feels like a treat, not like work. So, paradoxically enough, from time to time a good nightmare guarantees in the long run a better night's rest.

creative

48

To be and not to be

There is an even deeper layer in the story of the nightly competitor. What you're really trying to do by taking the detour of the Nightmare Competitor-scenario is to escape from your own paradigm – to jump over your own shadow. Every organization has an identity, a certain culture, a business model, a market, an image, a picture of customers and competitors. That functions in the daily practice very well: it is the "security" which makes it possible to transact business effectively. As side effects, we see rigidity, set patterns, rash reflexes, and they can, if the circumstances change, be counterproductive.

By creating the nightmare-scenario you can escape this. You rise up for a moment on your own terms and make room, space for a new paradigm. We call companies that do this well Conscious Companies. Those are the companies of the future.

The Myth

You're bombarded with it. Wherever you go, everyone's talking about innovation. You have university chairs in innovation, you have books and reference books on innovation, you have innovation managers, and even staff employee innovation courses. And even so, one hardly innovates.

There a lot of talk about innovation, including about what it really means. There's talk about who does and who does not innovate. There are even discussions about competition in innovation. What is innovation? As far as I can see, it's nothing more or less than a renewal that has been successfully adopted in practice.

Still, there are diehards who hold on to the definition of a technical renovation. As if innovation has been reserved for the world of techno nerds. Innovations that originated in laboratories are indeed often technical in nature. They are things made new — renewed. Take the hybrid engine, for example. That was once an innovation that is now being implemented with some success. And in this way there are a lot of technical innovations. But innovation covers an area much larger than what is expressed in the form of specific products. Like organizational innovations or

creative

# of Innovation

company innovations. The creation of a Free-Zone in Dubai has proved enormously attractive to all kinds of international companies. How does it happen that Dubai comes up with that idea and not some other country with the same goals? Namely attracting economic development. The Netherlands once reformed its tax system in a way that resulted in attracting tens of thousands of holding companies to establish headquarters there. Why did no other country come up with that idea? In the middle of the Golden Ages the Netherlands came up with a corporation that made it possible to set up large trade expeditions that carried goods and raw materials over the world's oceans. It was called the Dutch East Indies Company. And the year was 1602. Why did no other company come up with that idea?

Who will risk his neck?

Innovation, then, is to be found in all regions. Why then the discord about innovation? To innovate is in large measure to venture, as in "adventure". With a lot of risks involved. The Philips Company's Natlab has had its share of experiments that have failed. But the Natlab has always been a breeding ground for renewal. The same with Bell Labs and the Palo Alto Research Center. Unfortunately, there are few places like that

creative

left in the world. Community centers and playgrounds in which one can experiment, more or less unrestrained. In which one can arrive at original renewal. Originality is also an important element of innovation. Although I believe you can also innovate by coming up with clever combinations of existing developments.

Who has the guts?

You can even innovate by not at all being innovative, by just copying. Because something that for one organization is not innovative (because they have been doing it this way for years) may represent a true paradigm change for another organization. So copying innovation is possible, as well? If the one organization radically alters its sales strategy and as a result makes a tremendous impact on the market, that is a successful organizational innovation. But for another organization the same change may be nothing special, because they have been doing it like this for years. So to some degree innovation is a relative notion. But whichever way you look at it, technical or not technical, company or organizational, and paradigm change or not, enterprising or not enterprising, innovations are still a rare phenomenon. And why is that?

To innovate is difficult and scary. It requires enormous guts and entrepreneurship, and those are, after all, in scarce supply.

As already mentioned in the foreword, managers of organizations are being increasingly restricted by all kind of well-intentioned rules and regulations. Rules designed to assure integrity and transparency, Sarbanes-Oxley rules, and others. Rules that are meant to guard against swindlers who walk off with the shareholders' money. But those same rules further restrict those managers who are not very enterprising to begin with and who most need to innovate.

It's easy to talk and write about innovation, as I'm doing here. But innovation requires not just guts but stakeholders who will encourage risk-taking. In other words, shareholders who don't try to impose rules and restrictive controls, but put the emphasis on the long-term prosperity of the venture. But hold on a moment? Isn't it possible that the stakeholders in an organization might not support such a position, while the board might really prefer to wrap itself in the snug atmosphere of total control? Or is that really out of the question?

Put your money where your mouth is

I am convinced that an inspiring leader with a vision of the future can persuade every stakeholder in his company or organization that renewal, innovation, is in their own best interest. I am also convinced that such a leader can even persuade them to accept a year's losses in order to assure a more prosperous future. On condition that the story is authentic and with the proviso that the vision makes sense and inspires. Well yes, that's asking a lot. All the terms used in this book play a role here — terms like inspiring, authentic, visionary, persuasion, energy, and innovation. They all come together here. Because innovation is not so difficult as long as the preconditions are met. Are set up to include the very real possibility of failure. A relatively substantial budget, strong vision, willingness to accept risks, encouragement that includes accepting failure. That's a tall order. Certainly for those risk-avoiding managers it would be a nightmare. So it is simple, but it also has to be experienced, lived through, by the managers. Otherwise, nothing will happen. You can't give a kid a dime to buy a new bike. You have to put your money where your mouth is. Otherwise, we won't get anywhere internationally.

Failure permitted here

Sometimes you can find innovation in the most unlikely places. At one point I was giving a lecture to a group of about forty international top-managers. I was making the point — maybe too strongly — that most top managers do not innovate. But I touched a sensitive nerve with some of the managers. One of them was the head of a major dairy firm. He invited me to come by one day and take a look at his company's innovation programs. They had a separate building for the development of the most innovative programs. And those who worked there, while hoping to succeed, were allowed to fail. Failure was tolerated. The top man followed developments closely. He was truly on top of things. He had an exceptional interest in innovation. Because he understood it that it was on innovation that the future of the company depended.

On the other hand, just think of how many companies are led by financial engineers who think that a concern grows from takeovers. That, of course, is only make-believe growth. The real growth and expansion can only happen when a company provides new products and services well ahead of the developing market..., and thus when the company innovates.

A government agency surprised me recently by displaying an unusually strong innovative character. The administrator told me that every year the agency set up a very small initiative which then was given office space in a separate building. With a small budget and a clear-cut objective. Remarkably, the initiative's "offspring" was given explicit permission to attack the mother agency. Cannibalism was allowed. This caused a lot of

creative

panic within the bureaucracy, but every attempt to prevent the offspring from entering the market was blocked by the administrator. He visited the office of the innovative offspring daily. An amazing example from a government organization. Which, by the way, is now, as a result of this strong streak of innovation, very successful on an international scale.

But those small attractive successful initiative examples do not weigh up against the great lack of innovation found at most companies. And with the lack of an innovative culture found within most organizations.

Radiate!

Every self-respecting company employs the word innovation. But if you really start to look at what is being done about it in detail, and take a close look at the relationship between the investment in innovation and the total budget, it becomes very clear that in many cases it is a question of loincloths. It has nothing to do with a truly innovative culture, but serves as a substitute for the real McCoy. That may sound a little cynical, but it's just not good enough. Achieving innovation in a non-innovative culture is well nigh impossible. And so you could establish a Department of Innovation, but if you don't create the surroundings in which that department fits, it won't work. Companies that want to keep on growing in the long term and want to survive must take care that the total cultural innovation radiates. That innovation is being encouraged throughout and at all levels. That failing is not immediately reprimanded. That ideas are responded to in a constructive way. And not in a bureaucratic and risk-avoiding manner, which makes people very reluctant to bring forward another idea.

A firm that embraces innovation will at the same time become a pleasanter, more relaxed company. Because an innovative culture demands creativity, entrepreneurship and generates energy. Look at Google. Meanwhile, a company that embraces innovation will also become a lot pleasanter to work in and for. Sparkling and inspiring! If the United States were to invest in innovation on a really grand scale, might it be a pleasanter place to live in? Sure. Take a look at the little Dubai. There they invest for tens of millions in all kinds of projects all striving to realize a dream. So first there was the dream and the vision, and then the plans and the money. Knowing that America is much richer than Dubai, it should here also be possible in an uncomplicated way to create grand ambitions. Ambitions like Dubai's Palm Islands, built to boost the country's tourism.

To really arrive at innovation, several elements are required: the vision, the dream, the ambition all play an important role. And the freedom to be able to fail, which requires the removal of a few controls. We have to have the guts, the nerve. And still it will be difficult. So difficult that often there's more talk about an innovation myth than real innovation.

The Great Adventure
From Dreaming to Doing

People often ask me what is the most essential characteristic of an entrepreneur. And, as many authors have said before, I am also inclined to say that doing — the drive to DO — is centrally located within every entrepreneur. But I also think that only entrepreneurs know that there is another quality which is much more important and more crucial to their success. And that is perseverance. The ability to stay the course. Call it DOGGEDNESS.

Years ago I started my presentations by referring to the five D's. Deliberating, Dreaming, Daring, Doing, and Doggedness. Everyone knows them. How much fun it is, over drinks, to share all kinds of plans about things you would like to do. Writing books, building a house, restoring a castle, starting a company in cosmetics, or setting up a world-class golf tournament. And in this way there are of course millions of things to come up with that would be fun to do. And about which you can philosophize for hours with friends before you start. That stage of dreaming is immensely pleasurable. Especially if you do this in the environment in which the dream should take place. For example, during your vacation looking at the photos of houses for sale displayed in the windows of real estate agencies — that can be the beginning of a dream. A small step. The next is to open the door, to go inside and start up a conversation with the real estate agent. For most people, this may already be a bridge too far. To actually go with the agent and start looking at houses — for most, that is unimaginable. Still, it is fun to bring your dream a step closer in such a simple way. To see how that feels.

What's the right order?

You can also go to a lawyer and incorporate. A step that will allow you, later on, to start that dreamed-of business. Here, too, you are taking a step. But after the Dreaming starts the process of Deliberation, thinking of all the consequences. And, even as I write these words, I wonder, have I got them in the right order? Maybe I should start with Daring, and let the Deliberation come later. Because the process of thinking through a

Dream often opens the door to many lions and bears on the road, so that you may might want to close the door on that dream. And because, strange but true, most people are much better at thinking about the problems than of the opportunities. How come? I think the reason is that we've forgotten how to play. We've lost the knack. A child who builds a castle with Lego blocks, soon feels like a veritable knight. And believes that he is one. And that's something we've lost. We can no longer have that experience. If our Dream is, for example, to start up a cosmetics firm with branches world wide, that's a very nice dream. But as soon as we start to think everything through, as soon as we Deliberate, we discover a host of problems — either on our own or brought to our attention by others — and no longer see the upside, the advantages.

So let's put Daring first. Not Deliberating, just starting — with whatever. Sometimes I think that for an inexperienced entrepreneur it doesn't make much difference with what he or she starts. You have your Dream and let's hope that it is truly your Dream. Is it a very strong feeling that you may have suppressed for years, but that you really want to get on with? Maybe you've been thinking of starting up a software company for years, but then you start thinking about all the problems you might face — financial problems, the mortgage that has to be paid, what will happen if you give up your present job and so on. The list can be endless.

And so you never start?

You need Daring to go through the first phase. Maybe it's not such a crazy idea to start with Daring. And so — take a step. For example, go and have a serious talk with real estate agents about the possibilities of renting a space. Establish your company, design a logo, quit your job. Do something that poses a real a challenge. Take the first step. Like a bungee jumper — literally and figuratively — one step and you're out there, falling, and there's no turning back.

By taking a first step, you often kick-start a mechanism that sets things in irreversible motion. You have to go on. Deliberating, thinking comes later. I'm not making a case for rashly starting an enterprise. The experienced entrepreneur knows better. He will have gone through — more than once — the always-difficult phase that separates the dream from the realization of that dream. To my thinking, it's a magical phase. Sometimes the Dream is so beautiful that one would prefer to stay in that phase. And that is the reason that most, maybe 99 percent of the Dreams, get stuck in that phase. Because it is the most enjoyable, secure, and innocent phase. You can't win, you can't lose. Well, actually, if you really dream, and dream a lot, you may often win, too. At least, in your dreams.

Experienced entrepreneurs often quickly get down to the business of Deliberating. That is, they convert the Dream business plan in their heads (or sometimes sketched out on paper) into real plans. Because they are not that easily frightened by the lions and bears. Entrepreneurs couldn't care less about lions and bears. In fact, they tend to be so optimistic or opportunistic that they refuse to consider the possibility of encountering those beasts of the business jungle. If they meet up with them, they'll find a way to deal with them. Because, as my grandmother said, "people suffer most from the suffering they fear." There are innumerable problems we can come up with that will probably never happen. Or problems you cannot foresee, and they will happen. Let them happen.

So I am making a case here for the Daring instead of Deliberating. First Dare. Take a step and see what happens. In your surroundings and within your self. Develop a test product and start talking with potential customers. Because every time you want to realize a Dream, you will gain most of your knowledge from the reactions of the market. And because that process is so intimidating and new, it seldom happens.

Play-acting

Keep on Dreaming. But then pull yourself together and Dare. Take your Dream under your arm and go on the road. Gather reactions. Don't worry that your Dream will be ridiculed or dismissed. Something else, something new will come up. And Deliberating, that's something you'll be busy doing while you are already Daring. So you are doing something already. It's in the Doing that you acquire entrepreneurial skills. Because when you are at the stage where you've taken the first bold steps, the ball will start to roll. And then you don't have any choice: you just have to do.

But the reality is as hard as the Dream is beautiful. Suddenly, all those lions and bears leap out of the woods. Where did they come from? And your business plan, on paper it looks great. Magnificently divided into chapters. And your financial plan, which made a good impression on the investors. Everything looks great. Until it becomes reality, because then it turns out that your splendid plans have left a few things out. Your potential customers need more time to think matters over. The licenses you need haven't been issued. The test products from China arrive late (or not at all). Thousands of things you couldn't have thought of beforehand and which are not in your plans, they happen and you have to react. So there you are, in the phase of Doing, and that's where the misery starts.

And he pressed on

Most new enterprises fail within the first year. They are a failure, declare bankruptcy or they will become part of a larger Gestalt. For whatever reason, the Dream comes to a halt. The successes, because they also exist, have almost all been achieved by those who press on, despite failure. They continue to believe in the Dream. They fight to the bitter end. Exhausted, weeping from fatigue and or doubt, they don't give up. In the eyes of an experienced manager, such behavior is almost incomprehensible. Why don't you just quit and cut your losses? Why would you take out a second mortgage just to raise one more chunk of cash? Why not avoid these insane risks and just stop? Forget about the second mortgage. That would be crazy.

But still for an entrepreneur who believes in the Dream, that fifth D — Doggedness, the refusal to give up — is essential. Keep on going. Always keep on going. The first year of my very first company we experienced all kinds of nightmare surprises that would have ordinarily have shut the whole enterprise down long before the year was over. But by working sixteen hours a day, seven days a week, all problems were resolved and at the end of the first year we had ten people working with us. And every year after, things happened that would have made most people say, "That's it. We can't go on." There were many, many months when, in the third week, we didn't have a clue how we were going to meet the payroll. But every month we managed to meet it. Because the necessity to meet payrolls makes people creative. That kind of Doggedness that simply will not give up is frowned on by most professionals — those who watch from the sidelines. Bankers, well meaning friends, accountants, and other advisors. They're the ones who will urge you to limit your risk, take no chances, and so they are negative from start to finish. I'm not saying that all these advisors are charlatans. No. Being daring and dogged does not guarantee that everything will come up roses. Things can go wrong, and end in financial disaster.

But with almost every entrepreneur who succeeds in realizing his dream you will find that he or she has endured a time of despair through which they had to preserve in order to reach their goal. In the last book about Steve Jobs the moment at which he was almost bankrupt is described. His two companies — Next and Pixar — had almost gone belly up. And he himself had gone through almost all his reserves. But still, for some reason that the book does not make completely clear, he persevered. And his doggedness, his perseverance was rewarded. It was crucial, even if it could have led to three different bankruptcies. Doggedness, perseverance is what it is all about. Doing is easy. Think of a bulldog that won't let go. Doggedness makes the difference.

Scary stuff - starting a company

During a vacation in New Zealand a friend jumped from a bridge. Luckily, he was connected to a cord and that is called bungee jumping. I stood on the bridge, too, to take a look and see if I dared to make the jump, but that's as far as I went. The view was hair-raising and the plank you had to jump from was not very big. After his jump, my friend was surrounded by children who were very impressed and said it must have taken a lot of courage. Then they asked why I hadn't dared to jump. His answer is one I will never forget: "Leen does things that are a lot scarier — he starts up companies." To start up a company, that is truly scary. At least in the eyes of many.

What is entrepreneurship exactly and can every one do it? For me, the ultimate form of entrepreneurship is starting one's own company, with your own money. That last bit is very important, because the sense that you stand to lose everything often acts as a spur to enormous achievements. At the same, real entrepreneurs don't feel that the risk is real because they are so convinced that they will succeed that they shrug off the risk.

Return to a safe haven

But to focus on one's own money for a moment, and how important that is. In the dot.com hype thousands of companies were started with foreign money, money from investment associations. The money was being virtually thrown at those companies, and in large amounts. I am convinced that a lot of money corrupts. And you could see that very clearly in those times. The sense of proportion disappeared — and something else disappeared: the need to earn money from a customer. Just imagine, if you have millions in your bank account and with the blink of an eye you can get even more millions, there will hardly be any sense of urgency. Urgency to start doing business with the customer. You could see in that period thousands of so-called entrepreneurs. People who thought that they were entrepreneur, but in reality were only playing with other people's money. The feeling that that money — and in larger amounts, if you please — had to be paid back had gotten pretty much lost in the process. They weren't entrepreneurs, they were phonies. As soon as the bubble burst, they ran as fast as they could back to the safety of their full-time employment. But if you look carefully you can spot the survivors — the companies that emerged from the dot.com period stronger than before and now dominate the market. That's where you'll find the true entrepreneurs.

First — earn

To get a feel for how scary entrepreneurship can be, put yourself in this situation: you have three days to come up with the money to pay your employees' salaries. No salary for yourself — no, you have to go without so you can pay the others. At my very first company, I did not get paid for the first six months, because I had to contribute to the salaries of my ten employees. I did not want to create a sense of alarm. I just wanted things to run smoothly. I got that money back by the way, when the company was making a good profit. Not receiving a salary, or receiving less, has happened more than once. In fact, quite often. The rule I adopted was, paying began when earnings began. Not everyone understood that. Because most people look for security, and you can't blame them.

Entrepreneurs are optimists, that's one thing for sure. They see opportunities that others don't and they throw themselves into them, full of enthusiasm. They are doers. You can find thousands of would-be entrepreneurs at bars. Of the 100 ideas that are conceived at a bar, ninety will have been forgotten the next day. Something may come of the remaining ten or so, but finally maybe four companies will be started. Of which two will fail. By which I am trying to make the point that there is an important difference between thinking and doing. Of the 5 D's (Deliberating, Dreaming, Daring, Doing, and Doggedness), I think that the last one could be the most important one. Because after the start-up of a company, the entrepreneur often will be confronted with all kind of obstacles and with roller-coaster ride of ups and downs. Like the salaries that can't be covered, orders that at the last moment fall through, customers who go bankrupt, employees who quit. Press on and throw everything you've got into it. The die-hard entrepreneur believes in his idea and throws all his energy into it.

Sheer doggedness is therefore a very important component. More important than Doing, about which so many books have been written. Doing is the first step, but it's a relatively easy one. At least for entrepreneurial types. Because, granted, Doing is, for most people, an insurmountable obstacle. Starting up a company is an optimistic act, sometimes even opportunistic, working with a dream. A passion. And that passion may have no connection with money. Because that is also something strange; I am convinced that most successful entrepreneurs started their company because they believed in their own dream. The dream to start a music store, the dream to start a steelworks, the dream to create a pc for everyone. To realize that dream and make a big success of it, that's what concerns the entrepreneur. The money is a measure of the success. Not the ultimate goal. Not the driving power.

Looking back for a moment to the dot.com period and the bubble which followed: there were a lot of phony entrepreneurs busy chasing large sums of money. And what they had to do in return was not very relevant. It was not about the dream anymore but only about the money. I don't think that you can be a successful entrepreneur if your primary goal is making a lot of money. And if the dream of the new company is realized only after the money starts rolling in. Reverse the order and I do believe in it. To have a super idea and to make a terrific success of it… from which maybe you will earn a lot of money. But that is something else.

Bankruptcy as a learning experience

Entrepreneurs take risks. At least in the eyes of the bank. If a bank gives a loan to a company, it would prefer to do so if the company functions so well that the loan is actually not really needed. Often entrepreneurs say that "a bank provides an umbrella when the sun is shining." Banks don't look at it like that. No, they think they are partners in the venture and that they are taking risks, too. But let's say that it's not the banks' job to run a company. Because they would be using other peoples money, namely the depositors' money, the customers of the banks. And running a company with other people's money is not something real entrepreneurs like to do. They would rather not borrow.

But to take risks and to realize that things could go wrong — that all is just part of running a company. Of the fifteen companies and small businesses I have started, a few have become a big success, a few enjoyed mediocre success, and a few failed. Yes, that can happen. But I learned a lot.

In the United States, the bankruptcy of a company somewhere along the line will be taken as a plus in the context of your career as a whole. In Western Europe it's a whole different matter. And that's a pity, because going through a bankruptcy (or narrowly avoiding one) is such a valuable experience for entrepreneurs that one should almost try it. To experience the feeling, to go through it, and be prepared when setbacks occur. To get an advanced degree in Doggedness. Starting up a company you learn by stumbling and getting up again.

Talking about scary, the entrepreneur himself usually doesn't believe that he is doing anything very frightening. On the contrary, the entrepreneur believes steadfastly in the dream and sees the goal up ahead. Charges forward. Loaded with energy and drive. Optimistic and grabbing all chances as they offer themselves. If it can't be done one way, it can be done the other way, but continue it will. And that energy is boundless. In the first years of my very first company I worked seven days a week. Year after year. Saturday evening was a free evening and Sunday evening as well, but the rest was for the building of the company. Why? Because I reasoned that the only thing for free was my own time. And so I did everything myself. I did not buy any marketing strategy, but developed my own brochures and campaigns. I did not hire an accountant, but did the bookkeeping myself. I did not have any sales people, because I visited all the customers myself. By doing nothing but working and never spending any time at home with my family, I drifted apart from my family. So that side of the program was not pleasant. And I don't do things that way anymore. Finding a balance is something you also have to learn. You learn through experiencing a bankruptcy — in this case, a divorce.

Sharing success

Many entrepreneurs work themselves into the ground. The whole art is to keep things in proportion. Achieving a balance with yourself and your environment. Success will then be even bigger, because you'll be able to share it with others. Those who are still around and those who you are keeping an eye on, as an entrepreneur. Energy is clearly a basic characteristic of the entrepreneur. The energy that is generated by the passion, by the dream. That comes from yourself after all. And you can transmit that energy to others.

Is starting up a company scary? No, on the contrary. It is very enjoyable. To be an entrepreneur is a lot of fun. But if you examine it closely, you'll find that the process involves several elements that might scare many people off. But that is precisely what separates the real entrepreneurs from the wannabes, the phonies.

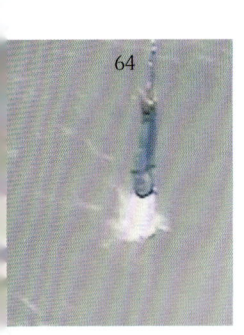

To start up a company with your own money is a bit like bungee jumping without a cord. The entrepreneur has no doubt all will be well, that he'll rebound. And as long as you have that kind of faith, starting up a company is not scary. But if you doubt that you'll land on your feet, the whole experience will be very different. Most people prefer to jump, with a very short tight cord. There's nothing wrong with that, but that's a different kind of bungee jumping.

The FUN of Sta

The Great Adventure

rting a Venture

This is going to be an ode to starting a venture. Or an ode in Praise of Folly? To describe how much fun starting up a company can be doesn't require a Hemingway. The freedom you get with starting a venture is phenomenal. But probably incomprehensible for others. In the eyes of others, entrepreneurs are just crazy.

Starting a venture can be defined simply as the making of independent choices, all on your own. You — and nobody else — determine your own success. It's a common saying that everyone is free to make his or her own choices. And that's perfectly true, in theory. But in reality it is a little too simple to say that people are free to make their choices when they are all tied up with their family, mortgage, loans, you name it. Of course, everyone has freedom of choice, but in most cases circumstances limit those choices. Maybe that is different with entrepreneurs. They're used to making choices themselves. They're used to being judged by their own success or failure. And they accept that fact.

When one of my companies, Escador, got off to a lightning start in the year 2000, and in no time at all had 200 employees, at first glance it seemed that there were many entrepreneurs among them. Escador at that time was the fastest-growing e-business company in the world! But the moment the internet bubble burst and the tide started to turn, a lot of those employees blamed everyone except themselves. And that, I think, is not exactly a characteristic of good entrepreneurs. The upside is yours, but also the downside. No whining, just keep on working. But I was going to discuss the fun of starting a venture, so we won't talk anymore about the phonies.

That feeling of freedom

The fun, where does it come from? Freedom and independence are two important concepts. Financial gain is another one, although I think that the financial element is more a reflection of the measure of success you enjoy as an entrepreneur. If you look at entrepreneurs who are totally absorbed by the realization of their dream, whether it involves the development of a building, the setting up of a camping ground, an ice cream parlor, or whatever business, the fun and the successful realization of the dream — are what really count. And out of these comes financial gain.

The Great Adventure

The way things are now, I don't think it's at all probable for the presidents of companies quoted on the stock exchange to show very entrepreneurial behavior. Entrepreneurial behavior always involves risks. Risks that in the eyes of the people who are not genuine entrepreneurs are unwarranted. And because that president has to deal with the executive board and a Board of directors, who aren't eager to sue for any reason at all, a risk-avoidance atmosphere prevails at all times. It really is not for nothing that a large number of companies have left the stock market.

Freedom and independence. The freedom to be able to decide that you are starting an adventure. That you want to invest a sum of money and an amount of time in something you believe in. I myself have done that fifteen times, with varying success. To believe in an idea and then create a company out of that. That gives you a real high. To start with nothing and to score the first customer. What a great feeling that always is. The first orders; it seems that other people think you've come up with a good idea. Fantastic!

The beginning of the end

When my first company started to grow, I thought that one should install a supervisory board. But by doing so I somewhat restricted my own freedom. A board of directors was created with more members, a management team. That was the second level of restriction. Finally we sold the company and a shareholder appeared who had the final word about all matters. The much-trumpeted freedom had all but disappeared — and that was also the beginning of the end. I've seen this happen more than once.

To start up a business is, to my thinking, the ultimate form of playing. As Marshall McLuhan put it: "Where the whole man is involved, there is no work. Work begins with the division of labor." People ask me how many hours per week I work. I am tempted to answer that I never work. But I also reply that I'm always working. I am always occupied with something, with venturing. That does not stop when I get into the car to go home. And it also does not stop during the weekend. My whole life is permeated with venturing, day and night. Luckily, my wife feels the same. If she didn't, this life in venturing would not be fun. Does it sometimes go too far? Yes, absolutely. Entrepreneurs are often egotists, usually brimming with enthusiasm, always preoccupied with their own ideas. Children are often put in second place. Preserving the balance between family and the entrepreneurial "me" remains a constant source of concern.

Yes, entrepreneurs are selfish. Selfish, because it can't be any other way. Always occupied with your company, your dream, your ambition to make the dream a reality. That makes for selfishness. In the eyes of others, yes. No doubt about it. You call that fun? Well, yes, for the entrepreneur who taps his energy from that drive. Not always for his fellow creatures, to whom he will pay less attention. The playing, all life long, is a fantastic way of life. But of course sometimes your own ideas drive you crazy. Because they keep on coming. It can drive you crazy. Because there are no obstacles to overcome until they are actually there. You encounter the obstacles and don't necessarily have to dream them up. That I call healthy opportunism.

Against your loss

To my astonishment someone once told me that "opportunistic" has a pejorative meaning, while I always thought it meant seizing an opportunity, the chance that offers itself, so I saw it as entirely good. Entrepreneurs always see new opportunities. In cases where others would have given up long ago, the entrepreneur forges ahead, stays the course. To persevere till the end, that is entrepreneurial. And as a result, the entrepreneur succeeds where others thought there was no hope of success. The fun of playing is always present. The freedom to come up with ideas that may seem far-fetched, wildly unrealistic. And that's why entrepreneurs are often called dreamers. Starting up a company does not necessarily have to be creative. To creatively think up a new idea does not mean that it can immediately be turned into a successful business. Entrepreneurs are able to separate the good ideas from the bad. To decide which idea has a chance to succeed and which does not. And you can always make a mistake. You get it wrong sometimes. Those who are bad losers should not play. And starting a venture is playing and playing is fun.

The Great Adventure

Where is the market?

The most bizarre experience I ever went through, at least where entrepreneurship is concerned, had to do with a boy who had inherited money and wanted to start his own company. He had come up with a great name and a super logo, found office space and furnished it with beautiful furniture. The most modern computers and gadgets, everything installed. I was envious of all those beautiful things, because at the time I was heading a small company whose headquarters were a small dressing table in my bedroom. Everything was ready for a great launch for the kid and the company could start up.

But when I spoke with him a few months later the situation of his company hadn't changed. What was going on? It soon became clear that he had no idea what he was going to do. Everything had been organized except the market. He didn't have any customers. I have to confess that I had been blinded for a moment by the kid's charm and the furnishings — everything organized, ready to go. And so I had never actually gotten around to asking him what exactly he intended to do. He had said he was so busy… Busy doing what? It later became clear he had been busy picking out the most beautiful furniture, the most efficient computer network, etc. But those were really the easiest parts. The most difficult part — the market — he had put off. He would worry about that later. You come across this quite often — this tendency to postpone. Why do many people who come up with ideas balk at entering the market? But at the same time talk about their ideas, make plans, draw up a prospectus, brochures? Everything ready to go, as long you don't have to actually enter the market…

Learn from the street vendor

Talk with the first street vendor you meet on the street and he won't understand this story. Because he lives and thinks street selling, his marketplace. He stands on the corner in the middle of the crowds, the market. And on the other side is the entrepreneur or manager who thinks about it, but doesn't dare to enter the marketplace. I don't think that the street vendor is afraid of his corner. Maybe sometimes he doesn't feel like standing there at his booth and maybe he's depressed by slow sales. But he is not afraid of standing on his corner. He doesn't know anything else. He is a part of his market corner. I've read that many successful entrepreneurs started out as street vendors. What a learning experience! Because from street vendor to shop owner is indeed a huge step, but anyone armed with the knowledge of that street corner has a big advantage. That's where the expression "street smart" comes from. From being out there. On the street, where the action is.

Thinking from the standpoint of the market he knows can give the entrepreneur a tremendous advantage. Always thinking from the market standpoint — using the market as your starting point. Therein lies success. Because all the trappings surrounding the market are actually unimportant. The starting point is always the market. Not the offices, the brochures, the written plans, the employee plans, and all the other details connected with leading a company.

And who is always right?

When I headed a company in virtual reality software in San Francisco, I

The Great Adventure

had buried myself in the complete administrative chaos of the company. Money flew out of the window and nobody knew exactly for what. That had to be stopped. The business of searching for customers and bringing in order with the best accountants in the Netherlands and the U.S. cost a bundle of energy, time, and money. And after months I came up with the brilliant idea to pay a visit to the users of the software, our customers. A little late, but better late than never. To start with, there were not that many customers. And the few customers we had were not prepared to pay a lot of money for our product, because in the meantime the competition, like Silicon Graphics, was giving the product for free with the purchase of a new computer. Well, that was an important discovery. Visiting our customers and discussing our products proved to be very useful in helping the company grow. In the process, it also became clear why we were spending our money on the wrong things. Visiting of the customers, the willingness to stand in the middle of the market is crucial. One of my managers told me at one point that he would have been glad to board up my office, so that I would never be there. So I would always be outside, in the market. Because that is what it's all about.

A lot of offices really should be boarded up . Because people have to be driven out into the market! Recently we started a program at a large international company. A program to train people to begin with the customer and with the market. That's so difficult — motivating people to get out into the market! Getting them to think from the point of view of the market is something that has been drilled into us in MBA courses and other programs. In which we have had exercises, for which case studies have been reviewed. But this almost always has been done within the safe confines of the university or company environment. Where the real customers are almost never present. Because to think like the market you have to be standing right in the middle of it. Just like the street vendor.

And that seldom happens. We are willing to think from the standpoint of the customer, but preferably from the safety of a company office or university classroom. Do you get the problem? To think from the point of view of the market but not from within that market. Not to have the real feel of the market and still to want to think from within it. That's the biggest problem. You'll find it in companies that can't grow anymore.

You're standing in the middle already

To think like the market you have to stand right in the middle of that market. And not weighing all kind of things with smart advisors and clever employees. It is very easy to kid yourself and to imagine that you are genuinely consulting with customers. But I know of only very few programs that have really been set up from within the market.

You can't see the trees from the forest. Where is that market? Where is our market at this moment? Oh yes, you are standing right in the middle of it, but you don's see it anymore. Management guru Tom Peters was asked at one point to set up a strategy program for Volkswagen. In his first conversation with the executive board of Volkswagen, he asked an important question: "Which of you has ever sold a Volkswagen to a real customer?" Dead silence. None of the members of the executive board had ever done that. "In that case, I will return after each one of you has at least sold one car. Goodbye."

That is the way it went, roughly. Hmm, the market. How many managers have themselves ever gone through the experience of selling a product or service? What are the objections of the customer and how difficult is it to sell something… You sometimes hear a manager say, "Unfortunately, we also have customers." Well, yes, it's said as a joke most of the time, but don't underestimate the serious undertone. Customers can be a pain, if you don't like dealing with them. Sales people in the fish market in Seattle (from Fish Tales, see also page 102) make a circus of their sales. Very nice to watch how they do it. Enjoying standing in the middle of the market. It can be done. Admittedly, some people do not like selling. But one shouldn't be too quick giving into that feeling.

I am the market

That's exactly what the Chief Financial Officer in a company told me recently in explaining why he saw no reason to participate in a market-oriented program. Because he was not involved with customers. Because he was just sending the invoices and at most he only had to deal with complaints about those bills. But he had nothing to do with the customers. You understand? As an organization, no matter what else you do, you've always got to deal with customers. In a one-man business that one man or woman takes the rap. In a two-man business you can divide the jobs, but you are still always involved with the customers. And in a company with 200,000 employees there will be 200,000 people who have to deal with the market. That's the way it is and always will be.

And where is the market? Everywhere, because we are the market. We think and feel like the market. We dream the market. Because we and the market are one and the same. Only then can a company work on its future.

The Great Adventure

Don't forget

the customers

I was stretched out on my bed one day while writing this book when it suddenly dawned on me that I was forgetting an essential aspect. The customer.

It's amazing how often organizations will spend so much time in strategy sessions at some dude ranch or remote island and all the talk will be about the customer. They'll take special courses, invite guest speakers, and hold impressive planning sessions on the subject of the customer. It's always about the customer, but rarely with the customer. Why is that? If you inquire what percentage of his or her time the CEO of an organization spends on visiting customers, the answer is likely to be embarrassingly small. Or close to nil. If you start thinking about it, you realize that much more time is spent talking about the customer than with the customer. Because with the customer is difficult.

Put them on your computer

Years ago Siebel Systems introduced a new system for the automated world – Customer Relationship Management (CRM). It seemed that the dual problem of customer contact and customer management would be solved by implementing this very savvy system. In the years after the introduction of Siebel, thousands of systems were quickly loaded with reams and tomes of customer-related data. The assumption was that customer contact was being addressed in that way and that the company was working hard at serving that customer.

This seems to me to have been one of the most important mistakes of recent years. I will concede that if your company has a lot of customers, a system that lets you store information about them is very handy. But to imagine that customer contact is being improved by the introduction of CRM systems is to delude yourself. I think that many organizations introduced the system to ease their sense that they were forgetting about the customer. That they were losing the customer. And using the system showed that they were thinking about the customer, learning a lot about the customer – but, again, not with the customer.

I once visited the headquarters of Siebel in Silicon Valley. The first thing you noticed was that right next to the main entrance a space was reserved for "Employee of the Month". Our company was a good Siebel customer, but there was no special place for us to park close to the entrance. All parking spaces were occupied except the one for the Employee of the

Month. He was apparently absent for that day. We parked in that spot because, thanks to our large contribution to Siebel's income, we considered ourselves "Customer of the Month". After our visit, we returned to the parking, where an angry man started yelling at us. He was the employee of the month and that spot was reserved for his car. Who did we think we were? This honored employee was disconcerted by our reply. "We are your customer and we pay your salary," we said, and left him standing there, looking bewildered. This employee did not embrace the Siebel philosophy of putting the customer first.

A flesh-and-blood customer

The customer. Many organizations see the customer as an abstract notion. A collection of profiles. It's easier to see things that way if you hide behind the fact that you could never meet those ten thousand customers in person. And then go on complaining about the lack of customer loyalty. Customers who know and feel that the company has no genuine interest in them return the compliment: they have no real interest in their suppliers.

They do exist, the little companies that really talk with their customers, that really know their customers. The small specialty shops, for example. The ones that are a little more expensive than the supermarkets. And, as a result, command more loyalty. Compare one of those small guys with a giant telecom, where all the fancy talk about customer loyalty and "developing the customer" goes out the window. The only connection the customer has with the company is talking with massive help desks. Furthermore, at these giant corporations discussions are limited to price competition. Which makes sense if the customer has no other choice. If it makes no difference to the supplier who the customer is, it won't make any difference to the customer who the supplier is. And no CRM system can do anything about that.

Slowly but surely, interest in establishing a real interaction with the customer is coming back. Re-establishing areas where the customer can be touched, not virtually but literally. After the large-scale cutbacks in the number of banks, shops, service desks, and so on, a movement has begun that is based on establishing physical contact with the customer. Feeling and seeing the customer, so that emotion and energy can be communicated, this is key to the solution of the loyalty problem. Because nothing human is unfamiliar to the customer.

Brrrrr, a customer

Where did the aversion of working with the customer come from? I think that one reason is fear of the customer. Also, many employees just don't have it in them or don't enjoy getting in touch with customers. But there is also a large group that has the potential for establishing a good relationship with customers, but hasn't discovered their talent yet. This might be the largest group.

Recently I discussed a new customer program with the sales director of a large company, in which we suggested that the more technically oriented employees should visit the company's customers. His first reaction was remarkable: "That's not going to help our bottom line." He meant exactly what he said, though he said it as if joking. But what he said was representative of what a lot of people think: that, if you want to sell anything to a customer, they have to be approached by commercial people. At the same time, it's widely recognized that customers would rather talk to someone who has real knowledge of the product than to be chatted up by a smooth-talking sales rep. Which is why I hold that the washing-machine repairman who is in constant contact with customers is better qualified to sell a new washing machine than the sales person in the shop. Those with the most credible, hands-on experience are the best sales people. In this connection, I heard of a musician who plays an instrument in a symphony orchestra who was hired part-time by a major company that sells musical instruments. Why? Because customers take people with his kind of experience seriously.

I would much rather discuss the choice of a new car with a friend who has some knowledge about cars than with a show-room salesman. Why don't we take all those lessons seriously and put them into practice when it comes to dealing with our customers?

What's gone wrong?

I have taken on companies whose problem is an inability to create contact with the customer. To start with, there's a fear of the customer. Fear that the customer will say No to our offer. This fear can be paralyzing. It can keep many salespeople pinned to the desks, petrified by fear. And this fear of a negative response leads to inventing all kinds of reasons for avoiding meeting the customer face to face. After all, it is much safer to sit in the office writing letters, sending out mailings, brochures, sales plans, and so on than to knock on a customer's door and ask to sit down with the customer, face to face.

Next to the fear of hearing the word "no," there is the dread of complaints. Every customer has issues, complains about products, complaints about everything. At least, that's what some people believe. The fear can really immobilize you. But a customer who complains is a customer who wants and is sending out sales signals. You are having a conversation with that complaining customer. He or she is a customer who wants something. The conversation represents an enormous opportunity.

I once organized a conference for my customers. There was a fee. It brought in some money and besides proved to be good marketing. You could say paid marketing. The conference was well attended and seemed to be a big success. But the day after the conference, a fax arrived – email did not exist in those days – from a very disgruntled customer. He had never attended such a lousy conference, he said. His whole day had been wasted. He indicated that he might refuse to pay the price of admission. I was furious and immediately drafted an angry letter. I would teach the cretin a lesson. But after I had written a few sentences, I decided to take a different approach. I started with the line: "I challenge you." I challenged him to the following. I would organize, especially for him, a new half-day conference, at our office, and we would go over the substance of the program. If, after this, he still held to his opinion that we had nothing to offer him, he would not have to pay the cost of the original conference. But if he was satisfied, he would be obliged to pay. Off went the fax. Less than an hour later, his reply fax rattled in. He was surprised, sounded rather pleased to be challenged, and accepted. A few weeks later he came to our office, spent the afternoon, and ultimately became one of our biggest customers.

A complaining customer wants something, has given the matter some thought, but is not satisfied. He has energy and passion, but it's a negative one. To turn that around is much easier than to generate it. So an angry, disappointed customer represents a big opportunity.

What shall I say…

Next to the big fears of getting "no" for an answer or having to listen to a complaint, there is also the common fear of not knowing what to say to the customer. This fear, as I've learned over the years, is much bigger than you would expect. This fear is closely linked to the mistaken assumption that hands-on people, like repairmen, aren't as well equipped to talk with costumers as salespeople. A conversation with a customer is much easier if you have learned to listen. And the customer will be eager to talk if you ask the right questions. When you ask unexpected questions. Listen and let the customer speak. And from which the customer tells you, it's usually easy to determine what he wants.

There are all kinds of other reasons why the thought of direct contact with the customer is frightening. The reason you hear most often is lack of time. Large organizations are the ones most likely to suffer from this affliction. The higher up in the organizational structure, the less time for the customer. Really insulting!

The customer should always come first — always, always. Easier said than done because often there are many more important matters, like reorganizations, high-level conferences, management consulting, or brainstorming sessions in some resort or other, or training courses or seminars, all of which stand in the way of direct contact with the customer. Because all those meetings are much more important than the customer from whom we earn our income. Just like that "employee of the month" at Siebel who had forgotten about his customers, that's how it is on a large scale at many organizations. External always comes before internal, that should be a golden rule. You should always have time for a customer. Now, and not tomorrow. Where does the core of the problem lie? Often with management, which should serve as an example. If the employees are constantly being summoned to attend extra meetings or meeting deadlines and setting up the CRM systems, the customer will always come last.

That is the reason for the title of this chapter. And it goes for me too. While writing this book, I caught myself making a big mistake: I was so busy describing all kinds of fun subjects that I forgot about the customer — for a moment. But a short moment isn't so bad, as long as the forgetting doesn't go on too long.

Of course, we never really forget the customer. The so-called forgetting usually stems from anxiety. People and organizations hide from their customers and get even more afraid. Because they aren't sure what those customers do and what they want. Which takes out all the pleasure of dealing with the customer. Because the customer should be an important source of inspiration. There is nothing as much fun as developing new things in collaboration with a customer. We call that co-creating. You could also say: co-creatively enterprising. Each party inspires the other. And you develop an iron bond. No sales pitch can compete with that.

Hey, Buddy:
business

Get me some new

We want growth. Growth in turnover and growth in profits. But it's a pity that the emphasis over the past few years has been on improving efficiency, cost cutting, control, Sarbanes-Oxley rules and regulations, and the like. Most companies aren't in the mood for building new business. They're just hunkered down trying to maintain the status quo or cutting back. It's not going to be easy to turn things around and get back to entrepreneurship.

During my days as an accountant, the one thing I couldn't stand was the fact that the past was so neatly plotted out, controlled, and analyzed. While it's the future, not the past, that you really want and should be dealing with. That's why I finally had to say goodbye to that profession and throw myself into building up companies. Don't get me wrong: financial control is needed and desirable, as long as it is not going to be a guiding force in management. And that's exactly what's happened in many companies. There may be a reason for this, but it's poison for entrepreneurship.

To attract trade

It's said that managers who want to boost profits, lower the costs. That may prove to be a successful policy when a company is just starting up, but everyone knows that its usefulness is only temporary. Entrepreneurs, on the other hand, see boosting sales as the way to increase earnings. Hey, buddy: get me some new business! If this sounds a little sarcastic, it's for a reason. All too often, people divide companies into two kinds. Those that for years have held back on expenditures (and have only recently discovered that they've gone too far) and those that are almost entirely focused on increasing sales. Only a company that wholeheartedly pursues increasing turnover has a chance to survive. Those who hope to get anywhere by cutting costs and imposing controls don't stand a chance.

Add a little fertilizer

Okay, then, new business. The turnover has to start to grow. How are we going to achieve that? I'll keep on hammering on this one point for a moment — the important cultural change that must be made from the managing, financially directed style to the entrepreneurial, creative style. There's a real difference there — a head-on collision.

The goal is to develop creative units in the company without, of course, abandoning cost control. Because that would be asking too much and dangerous besides. First of all, the people who own the company. They have to be inspired to consider the company's growth potential. Preferably, a growth based on existing customers. But the staff has for years been trained to think in terms of cost and how to keep them down. The spirit and daring required to come up with new ideas is gone and can't be brought back easily.

It is essential, then, that top management demonstrates, in words but especially in deeds, that they are serious about the transition to a culture that emphasizes growth. By setting an example themselves. By making it clear that there will be room for a certain amount of chaos and failure. Because there's no doubt about it, increasing a company's profit by increasing turnover is much harder than increasing the profits by cutting costs.

Hand me a crowbar?

Internal and external. Another important difference whose impact we need to understand. Cutting costs and imposing controls are always a purely internally directed process. A lot of grand talk within the security of the walls of an office, lots of talk and more talk — resulting in a master plan that will save the company. But that's all internal, developed within. Centralize purchasing, make departments more efficient, give people the pink slip, outsource general and technical support services, long-term investment decisions and the like are all being driven from the inside, and often have nothing to do with the outside.

External is the market. To reach the market you have to get out of the office, get in your car, off to the customer. And that is really difficult. Because the customer has known you only as a supplier who has been trying to economize. And who previously had no real interest in him at all because the company's only concerns were internal. So the cultural shift we want to bring about — putting the emphasis on growth — has important consequences, both for one's employees and for the customer. Those two groups, then, have to be convinced that this transformation is for real. But you can't just one day announce that from now on "the customer is going to be central to our business" that would just make customers laugh. A joke. Why should the customer believe us? An already satisfied customer might take you seriously, but that's not the one you're after. So it's the job of the initiators of the new strategy to prove that the transition from internal to external is serious. That you mean it. And you have to do more than talk about it. Something has to happen.

Great! We are going to do something. Oh oh. Suddenly we stumble over the existing structure of the organization. The one we have tightly riveted and bolted together over the past few years to comply with all the rules and regulations. To prevent fraudulent accounting in this company. A phantom sense of security has been built up. All employees have taken courses in ethics. Accountants are earning a ton of money overseeing all the control systems. But the structure stands. And within this structure we are going to try to encourage employees and customers to work together, to do something different from time to time. Something that doesn't fit within the existing organizational structure. Which is playful and more creative. Which requires faster response to the market. A response that can't be held up until we get the thirty-eight signatures required before a suggestion can go anywhere. How are we going to solve this?

So, show me
"Hey, buddy: get me some new business!" I chose this as the title for this chapter because it often seems that people think that the desire for growth is as easy to fulfill as ordering a cup of coffee — or a boss's order to cut costs. And that is a fundamental error in judgment. To create a culture in which creative entrepreneurship is appreciated and creating chaos from time to time is permissible, a culture in which you can do things that normally are prohibited or were thought to be impossible is very difficult and requires both courage and time. And it requires something

more: examples, examples, examples. I once thought that the transition in culture from internal to external was a process solidly based on statements. But documents, prescriptions, and instructions don't help. People want proof, evidence — they want to see something. The customer wants to see that his questions or problems are really addressed, and employees want to see that they are allowed to spend time on customer-directed projects, which may not yield immediate results. The truly physical seeing and feeling is a very important aspect of this transition from internal to external. Not words, but deeds. Admittedly, those actions may also have occurred within an internally directed culture. Thus, there is usually no shortage of energy. It just seems so unnatural to hear the financially oriented top manager, who was responsible for constructing the financial control structure, put forward a totally new message. It can be done, but it still feels strange. And with all we know in the back of our heads about authenticity, about what's genuine and what's not, an organization knows unerringly when a message of change is only talk. The customer knows, too. And so it's bound to fail.

Imagine that we have everything under control and have been communicating with customers and employees and, besides, have built up some flexibility in the organizational structure. Then we can start to really create a new business. Which by the way we can also buy (by taking over a company), and often it will be a better fit with the internally directed culture. Because after the takeover comes the integration, with the savings that go with it. This is a process we are used to. This kind of growth — which comes with acquiring another business — and not self-generated or organic growth, seems again to be much easier. But the catch with mergers is always the actual integration. Not the financial and organizational integration, but the integration of cultures. Yes, of course, it can have some value in the eyes of the stockholders, but it's not necessarily pleasant for the employees. But don't despair. There are also some very successful growth models that grew out of takeovers, as Cisco or Google, for example, prove.

New business always has to be directed toward the customer. And better yet, preferably guided by the customer. The customer decides what he wants. And we listen. That's the key. And this again is difficult, because internally driven organizations are usually not accustomed to listening. The customer will spontaneously indicate what his needs are, and show the good listener possibilities for new business. To start the process of generating a new business, we must start the flywheel. It's a process that may be quite bumpy, with successes and failures along the way. The sharing of both is important. And it is important that failures be accepted.

The Great Adventure

To get the customer to work with you, it is also immensely important to explain that there are areas of uncertainty, that you don't know everything. Because the customer also would like to have a more congenial supplier who really wants to help him.

Cuddle your baby

It is important that the first customer-initiated projects that will generate volume are carefully supervised. By the customer and by the company that produces it. Constant monitoring and painstakingly close attention are required. Because it's all new and the organization has the DNA within itself to frustrate the tender new projects. We need to be aware of this, because otherwise we cannot combat it.

Slowly, step by step, learning to walk. That is the process of creation of a new business. From internal direction to external. From costs to turnover. Very difficult, this business of generating something new.

To be co-creative, that is: to do business with customers in a creative way. The customer is thus the motor of the process of transformation, not the internal blueprints for change. This way you work from the outside to within on changing the organization and you let the customer help in the creation. Co-creative entrepreneurship. You become known to the customer, transparent and also close, because the customer feels connected. Così, which is Italian for "thus". But it can also be an acronym for Co-creative entrepreneurship and Sparkling Innovating.

88

The Great Adventure

Managers
and entrepreneurs

The Great Adventure

What's so attractive about entrepreneurship? At the end of my study in business economics, my grandfather, who in my eyes was a great entrepreneur, strongly advised me never to start my own company. No, he said, I should stay for a long time with Philips, the giant Dutch electronics firm that had just hired me. My being hired by Philips was apparently an enormous achievement. At the time, I didn't understand his advice. Because in my eyes nothing could top becoming an entrepreneur. That's just the way things go sometimes.

So, what's so special about entrepreneurship? Why do managers feel insulted when I point out that they are not entrepreneurial? Why are they also so eager to be an entrepreneur? Is it more macho to be an entrepreneur rather than a manager? Or are the two actually the same? I didn't think so. Entrepreneurial managers do exist, or managing entrepreneurs. The latter is considerably more difficult than the former. There is a real difference between entrepreneurs and managers. When I started my very first company, a vice-president was working there at one point. He was hired after the company had gone through its first year and was showing some stability. He resigned from his other job and started working for us. But I'll never forget the heated discussion — you could call it a row — we had about entrepreneurship. He considered himself an entrepreneur and I thought of him as, at most, an entrepreneurial manager. He believed that he had taken risks when he took on the job with us, while I felt that there had been no entrepreneurial risk anymore at the time he came aboard. Not important such a discussion, but quite typical. Because, clearly one is eager to be an entrepreneur, but also, and more to the point, because there is such a difference in the way risks are perceived. I would like to discuss those risks for a moment. But, first, in all honesty, I want to report that the vice-president in question later started his own company. So, he was an entrepreneur after all...

A kiss for the bureaucrat

Risks are an important part of the life of the entrepreneur. But risks are relative. What one person sees as an enormous risk is, to another, of minor unimportance. One will do all kinds of market research before he introduces a product, the other will act on his gut. Much faster, but also with a chance of failing. Incidentally, market research often offers only a sort of phantom certainty.

My first company, Bolesian, was in the field of artificial intelligence, also called AI (Artificial Intelligence). We started with a simple business plan in 1986 and wanted to get our funding together before we really got going. Something on the order of a hundred thousand dollars. So we visited a number of venture-capital companies. There weren't that many at the time, but there were a number of companies that would occasionally provide venture capital, so long as no risks were involved.

Nobody would give us the money we needed because we couldn't hand them a thorough market study showing how big the market was for our product. The problem was just precisely that there was, as yet, no market. In our heads, there was — or there would be. And this later turned out to be true. But the fact that we said that, at present, there was no market made the risk unacceptable for the bankers. And so, it proved impossible to get funding from them.

Risk. Entrepreneurship. The two are almost synonymous. Certainly that's so in the eyes of the non-entrepreneur. Managers try much harder to avoid risks. Or at least to keep them under control.

Wanted: bigshots with guts

Actually, I am a big fan of good managers. They clean up the mess, the chaos, that, in their eyes, I create. The chaos created by the entrepreneur. The founder of Apple, Steve Jobs, is in my eyes a great entrepreneur. Always looking for possibilities to enlarge the turnover. Furthermore, he goes head-on against every obstacle that comes up. That's what entrepreneurs do, to create turnover and growth in an environment where others don't see any hope for growth. And growth is essential for every company. Where capable managers boost profits by cutting costs, entrepreneurs boost profits by increasing turnover. And let's be clear about that and remain clear about it: increasing turnover is very difficult. Especially in a stagnant market. It requires guts, insight — in short, entrepreneurship. And only a few have that.

It's often said that you can't find entrepreneurs inside companies because they would have few opportunities to exercise their talent. I wouldn't go that far. What I am sure of is that an entrepreneur can't survive alone in his or her own company. I think that there are entrepreneurs who can stand it for a while within a larger organization. But I don't see a true entrepreneur spending his whole working life inside a multinational company like IBM, for example. At most, an entrepreneurial manager could do that.

The Great Adventure

Characteristic entrepreneurial qualities such as the willingness to jump on opportunities as they arise, guts, risk-taking, investing one's own money, and daring to pay one's self out of revenues — there's just no room for them in big, well-ordered companies. Even though you can find a few examples of big corporations that are making an effort to recruit and hold onto entrepreneurs. Back in the eighties, that was called **Intrapreneurship** — exhibiting entrepreneurship within the organization. But the problem I've always had with that is that those same large organizations were very shy of taking risks. Besides, it was always difficult to enable the entrepreneurs to enjoy the profits of their successful projects. In short, it was always what you might call a handicapped form of entrepreneurship. It was playing Mommy and Daddy, not the real thing and not realistic.

Entrepreneurs sometimes take unwarranted risks, at least that's how others see it. They mostly don't see it themselves that way, because they see where this risk-taking will lead to — the goal. But such "unwarranted" risks are often not acceptable for the large companies who do the most talking about Intrapreneurship. When Bolesian was sold to Cap Gemini, we had a small affiliate in Boston. The staff was tiny — a man and a half, a desk and a telephone — but it made a profit. At a certain point the boss of Cap Gemini came to me and said I should close the Boston operation. When I asked why, he replied, "Because. Because I am the boss here." The risk was apparently too great. I closed down the affiliate and, shortly after handed in my resignation. My entrepreneurship was being too restricted.

The golden combination?

Entrepreneurship and managing are two fundamentally different roles. But still they need to co-exist, side by side. They are roles that can't help but create collisions. Entrepreneurs are often loners, selfish, tyrants, dictators, visionaries, dreamers, and fighters, while managers are team players, organizers, planners, realists, and risk managers, or risk controllers. But energetic entrepreneurs and respected managers have a few things in common as well. Both can inspire, both can lead, both fight, and, if things are going well, they have the same goal in mind. So they can be a good match. But often there will be a collision or it will end in a collision, as in the case of the entrepreneur Steve Jobs and the manager John Scully (originally from Pepsi).

That's the reason that you don't find both types at the top at many companies and organizations. The entrepreneur and the manager are two types that are difficult to combine and, in most cases, incompatible. But both are needed. Because you want to grow and, at the same time, maintain a level of control over the whole operation.

What surprises me is that the companies dealing with stagnating turnover don't deploy many more entrepreneurs in the battle for more volume. In my eyes, the distinctive characteristics of the entrepreneur are far too seldom used. It's very rare that a company will actively recruit entrepreneurs, who will be apart physically as well as organizationally. How many companies are plodding along in stagnating markets? They try to disguise the situation by a refined system of cost controls, as a result of which profits stay relatively level. They lack the daring to take on limited risks beyond the borders of their own company. Or they leave new initiatives designed to increase volume to managers who just happen to be available. And often they were available because they simply aren't the best. Few dare to assign their best people to high-risk projects.

The Great Adventure

It's for good reason that I put growth projects at the border of the parent organization. Or next to it. Or completely outside of it. That's the safest. With the proviso that the turnover of the "mother" can be completely cannibalized. Everything is allowed in the battle and the search for more volume.

On the borderline

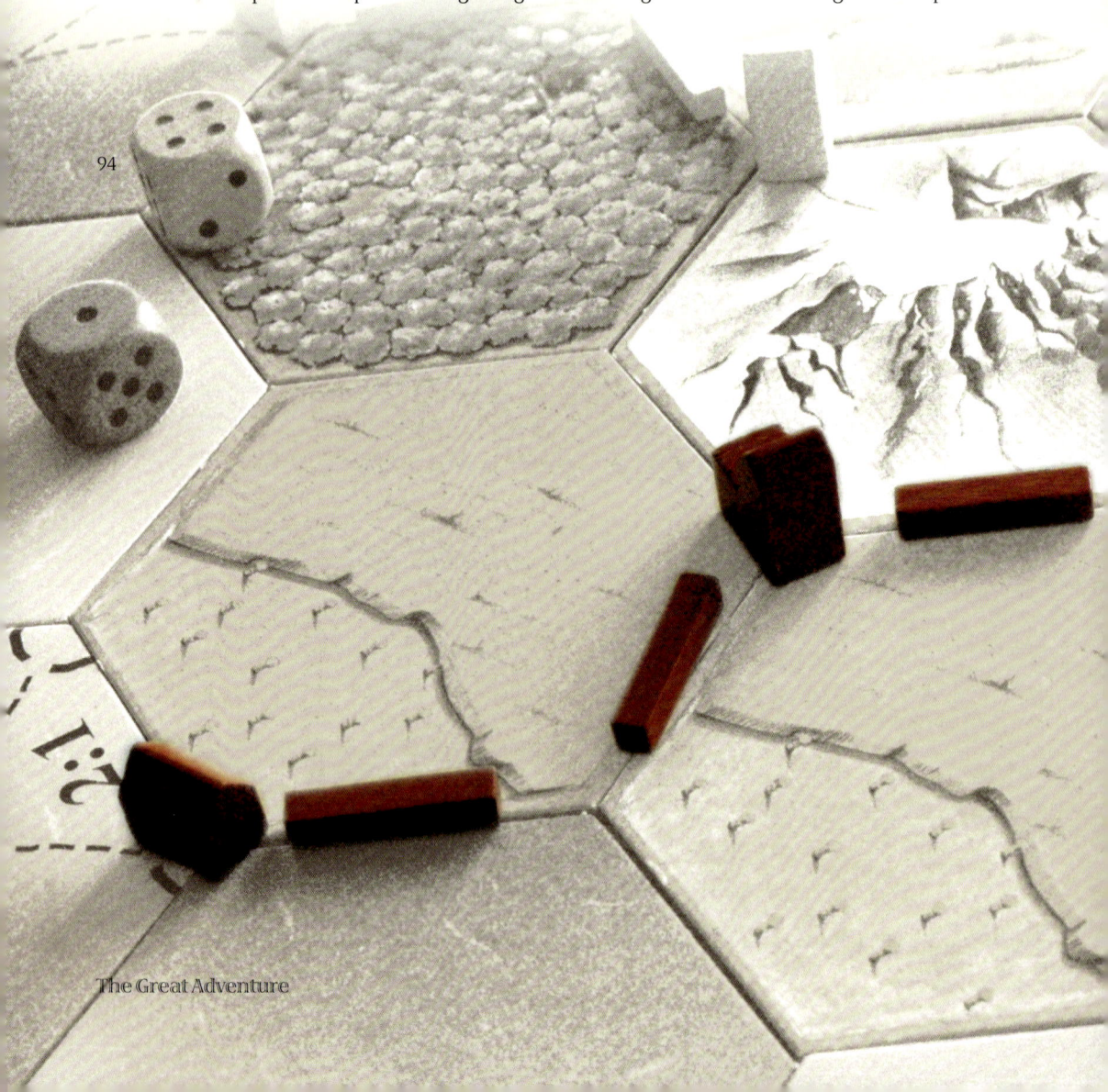

No, you hardly ever see this form of entrepreneurial effort. Look at Cisco, which for years experienced enormous growth by buying a whole string of small companies. As a matter of fact, most of the entrepreneurship took place outside of Cisco. And at the moment that the new technology grew to full stature and became useful for Cisco, there was a takeover. Entrepreneurship was being bought. How long the leaders of the gobbled-up companies could endure inside the corporate culture of Cisco, I don't know. But that's one way. Then there's TNT, which has a fund that the company uses to invest in both internal and external initiatives, which are likely to contribute substantially to the company's coffers. The name of the fund is Logispring. Entrepreneurs are being placed mostly on the outside or on the border of the company. There they can still flourish. Where they can still be creative and still take risks. If a project looks likely to succeed, the big investment company TNT will take over. If not, too bad — the project will be abandoned. So this is another route to take. Admittedly, even such a fund is a risk, but a controllable one.

Sparkle!

Business Dialogues

What steps can a company take to make it truly sparkle? Every situation is different, of course. Nevertheless, we can define a number of steps that will promote the process. Let's start with the golden rule: the customer must always be the prime focus, the central point to all considerations. Easier said than done, because although most employees of an organization can devise strategies designed to put the customer first, the very need to do so is counterproductive to the process of reaching the desired objective. It's a sign that the customer had never previously been the central focus. Putting the customer at the center of all considerations would seem to require us to consult the customer regarding every last detail. Meanwhile, to make the customer truly central, we will have to find out in what way the customer wants to assume a central role, and this can be done only through face-to-face contact, person-to-person. Only then can we start thinking as an organization about how to proceed. It's all very complicated.

To really see and feel who the customer is and what he or she wants. But there are also cases in which one never sees the customer. In such cases, you still have to hustle. Take any federal agency — the U.S. Department of Transportation, for instance. How often do people employed by a department of that size actually see a customer? Besides the fact that the people employed by the department are themselves "customers" (they can't get to work without using a highway), there is no good mechanism to allow others who rely on the nation's highways to communicate with the supplier. And those 'others' include virtually every American car owner. Or, again, take the example of the U.S. Postal Service, which has almost all Americans as customers, but has no efficient means of contacting all of its customers. Do you communicate with your local post office via the person who delivers your mail? No, you don't. But how else, then? So the fact that you can easily define your customers does not automatically mean that you can communicate with them. Let alone that you can really make the customer the prime focus of your concerns and actions.

No story, no customer

And what is meant exactly by making the customer central, the focal point? Does it mean that Vodafone, for example, should ask its customers what their precise needs are? Or whether they should lower the rates? No, making the customer the central focus point is more subtle than that. The customer has to get the feeling that he is been taken seriously, and that is difficult. The customer has to develop a feeling for the supplier by means of genuine stimuli. As a result of which the supplier gains standing, a special relationship, with the customer. A relationship based on more than price and product alone. The customer is looking for a story and a feeling. As previously mentioned, organizations that have no story will not survive in the long run. And that really goes for all products. When an office cleaner not only empties the wastebaskets but also waters and sprays the plants, this will be noticed by the employer and remembered. As a result, the service of a commodity immediately shifts to a different level, for which the customer is willing to pay a little more. Or the UPS man who is just a little friendlier and more attentive and thereby creates a small bond with the recipient. Nicer for the customer, but nicer for the UPS folks as well.

Granted, working with very large groups of consumers is fundamentally different from working with relatively small groups of customers. In the United States, there are hundreds of companies that serve many thousands, or hundreds of thousands, or millions of business customers. For such companies the so-called rule of eighty-twenty frequently applies. In other words, about 20 percent of the customers account for about 80 percent of the turnover. You would think that those organizations would concentrate on the 20 percent that bring in the most business. And to get to know that group thoroughly. But often that's not the case.

What do we want to know...

Knowing and knowing are two different things. Knowing what is happening with your biggest customers and knowing what's going on in the heads of their executives are totally different. Reading and hearing what is happening with your important customers (and putting that on paper in customer reports and plans) is routine operating procedure. Sometimes this is done very professionally and the details gathered are very impressive. But truly knowing what factors play a decisive role in the decisions made by your most valued customers is a whole different story. Why is that? Plans being made about customers often originate from the services and products the organization can provide. And those plans seldom originate from the customer's wishes and business ambitions. Many plans start with what the customer buys now rather from what they might buy in future.

Because it's usually the top executives of the company who make the policy decisions, it is essential to figure out what the customers' dreams and ambitions are. And these are rarely spelled out in the customer's plans and projections. These are things that, as a rule, the customers keep to themselves. One reason being that some organizations can't even allow themselves to do that. Market rules may be an inhibiting factor. So interaction with your big customers is likely to be more difficult than at first it might seem.

On the other hand, people often welcome a chance to talk about their ambitions and dreams, even though they are seldom asked about such things. So when a customer feels at ease, he may open up about what motivates him or her and what his or her hopes are for the company. Business Dialogues are a powerful means to create a super-strong bond with your biggest customers. Business Dialogues are not just talks with a customer. No, they are carefully prepared meetings between supplier and customer at which three or four people from each side are present. In total, about eight people who truly want to share their dreams and ambitions. And such dialogues are impossible without preparation. It requires a number of in-depth interviews preceding the dialogue, with one-to-one conversations designed to figure out what's really at stake. Thus, searching for authenticity. And the search for authenticity cannot be rushed. It takes time, plenty of it. Pull up a chair. Sit down. But imagine that finally both sides can share that essence with each other in a morning-long meeting. At that point you will not only have created a real bond, but the prospect of bigger business deals will open up quite naturally. Big business deals, because you are talking about matters that are genuinely important. It's no longer a matter of simply supplying familiar services and products that you know from each other. It is about really coming together.

In search of essence

Thorough preparation for Business Dialogues is not common practice in the The West. Why? Because the process is so time-consuming. It takes time and energy to acquire in-depth knowledge about your customer. But if you know who the 20 percent of your customers are who supply you with 80 percent of your turnover, it is certainly worth your while to have conversations with them of this kind. In the last few years I have organized Business Dialogues with about a hundred-and-fifty large international companies. It was a zany experience. Because in advance of those hundred-and-fifty consultations, we had to conduct at least five hundred in-depth interviews to be able to figure out what the core interests of the participants were. And one thing is for sure. This was not the kind of information you could find in annual reports or in other documents. One really had to search for it.

What an enormous amount of energy was released in those hundred-and-fifty Business Dialogues! Because, in almost every case, the participants enjoyed the sessions. Pleasant and open, genuine and authentic. And that is something people appreciate. After all people are glad to talk about their dreams and ambitions and they have too few occasions and opportunities to do so. The busy calendars leave too little free time and are controlled by the routine craziness of another day at the office.

Business Dialogues are an ideal way for organizations to get to know their big business customers better. Or, better said, they are an optimum means of fully understanding their customers. By being receptive to the essence of your customers, and by responding seriously to what you find, and by entering deeply into it, and, finally, by connecting your customer's concerns to your own you will have arrived at the ideal way to place the customer in the center. You will be able to look at things from the customer's point of view. And not only is that very pleasant, it will also result in an enormous amount of new business. And that is inspiring for the customer as well as the supplier. It produces meetings that sparkle, that contribute creatively and entrepreneurially to the growth of business. And that is fundamentally different from maintaining the status quo. It is working together with the customer on a new relationship. Which will be maintained longer than a normal relationship with a customer. And that's exactly how it should be! Or, in other words, cosi, as the Italians would say.

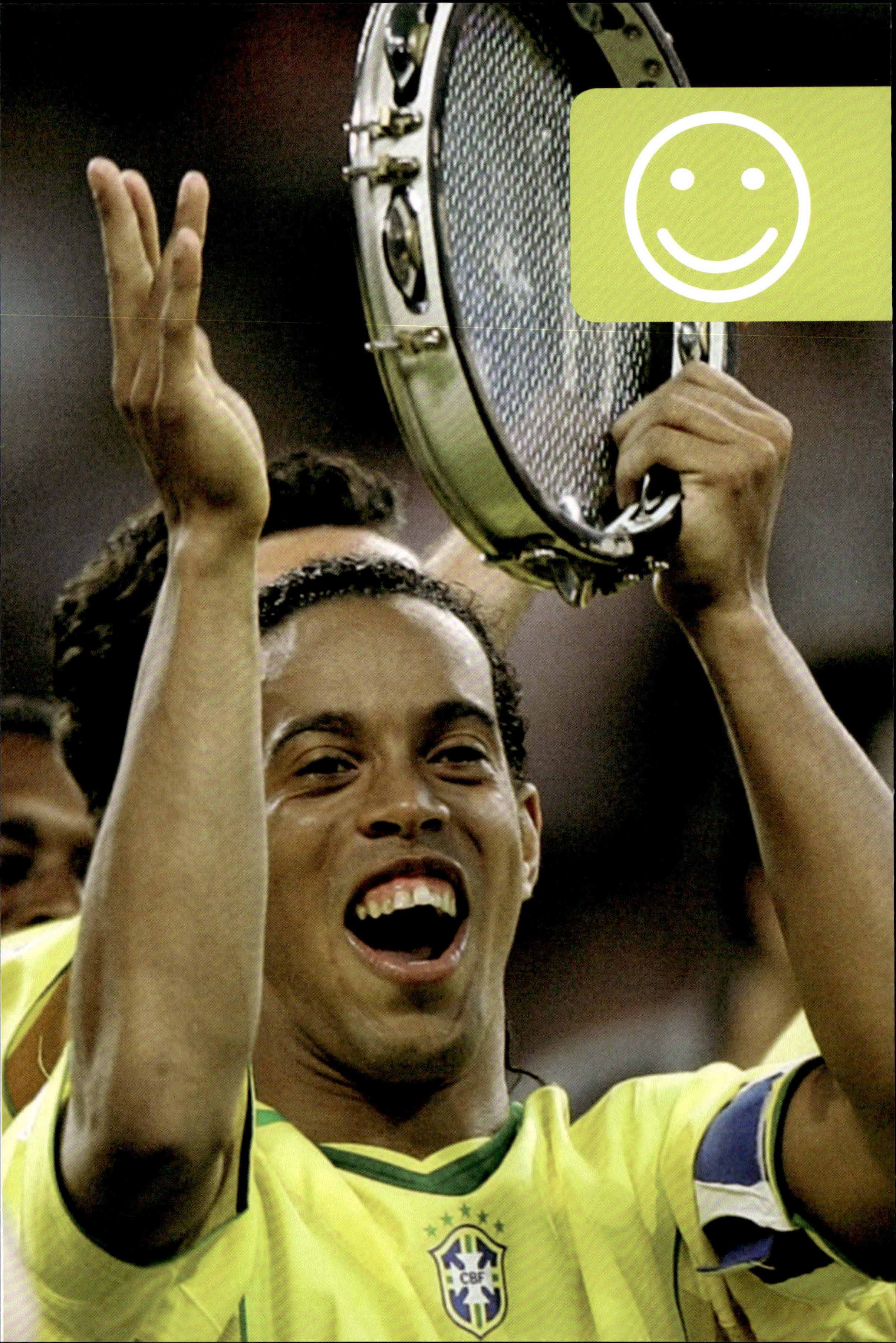
CBF

Enjoy
the job

On average, a person spends 75,000 hours at work. For some, those hours will be a grind; for others, a pleasure. It all depends on how you look at your work. As a task that keeps you occupied from nine to five. Or as an environment that provides an opportunity to do things you enjoy doing.

If you regard work as a game rather than as a struggle, it really isn't work anymore. It's simply an enjoyable way of spending time. And it's not hard to make a game out of your work. There are lots of ways. For instance, with every decision, you can ask yourself; What would I really prefer to do? Not, How can I make the most money? Or, What's the fastest way to get to the top? The reckless pursuit of wildly ambitious goals that you set for yourself generally ends up in disappointment. If you choose challenges and pleasure, you'll wind up satisfied and successful. If you set yourself the goal of getting the maximum amount of pleasure from your work, you will achieve the best. Pleasure in work comes from being challenged. And from the satisfaction you get when you attain your goals. You yourself, your colleagues. And, not least, your clients.

Sitting in a cubicle

Several years ago I was sitting next to a very successful street market vendor in his big Mercedes. We were driving through Rotterdam and had to stop for a traffic light. The vendor bent slightly forward and peered up through the windshield. Suddenly he pointed his finger and said, "You see that office building? Every morning people go in and leave again at five. They read the newspaper, drink coffee, and spend the whole day in a little cubicle." The light turned green and we continued on our way. The message didn't dawn on me immediately. Because at the moment that I was sitting with him in his car it was my own ambition to land a job in one of those buildings. Only later did I realize what he was saying in his sarcastic way about the "little men and women," as he called them, who sat there doing nothing. But apart from his dismissive attitude there was the observation that the free boys, entrepreneurs like himself, could make their own decisions, while a lot of people in that big office building had long since lost any sense of making their own choices. They just "troop in and out every day."

It's sad to think of the great mass of people who, with their brains set on zero, sit for hours in traffic jams and then troop into a building where they will spend eight long hours. Without ever asking themselves why. Or whether their lives could be totally different. Is this an elite thought or could it be applied at every level in the work process? Could not just executives but also people in the service sector have such thoughts? And, suppose they do, could they act on them? I am convinced that everyone, on every level, can think about his or her own situation and can effect change. And that seriously considering the issue of what gives one pleasure in the workplace is not just a matter for the upper echelons.

An amusing book that I read recently tells the story about a fish market in Seattle and the way the fishmongers deal with their customers. By establishing personal contact with their customers, through jokes and personal remarks, they have become a big tourist attraction, and sales have gone through the roof. They put on a great show. A whole raft of management theories have been built on the basis of fish market successes.

Then there's the story of Fred the Mailman who made a game of the job of delivering mail. These stories reinforce my belief that creating pleasure in your work is something for all levels in an organization. But the myth that you can never change your own situation, that decisions are entirely in the hands of "the Boss" or "the Management," is deeply ingrained in the modern worker.

Everyone for himself

While people may have different ideas on the subject, everyone agrees that enjoying one's work pays off in every way. Why, then, is there this anxiety that having 'fun' is not cost-effective? Sometimes I get the feeling that everyone, especially the managers, acknowledge intellectually that enjoying one's work is very important, but they don't follow up on it. Or maybe from time to time they will put together some patchwork project designed to improve relations with management. Employees treat their company the same way the company treats them. Just as people do outside the workplace. Companies that show no respect for their employees and don't stand by them will get employees who will feel no obligation to stick with the organization. It's only logical.

In the nineties I led a company in San Francisco. It didn't take long to realize that there was a total lack of loyalty to the firm. When I asked members of my management team how they accounted for this, they said the basic reason was because, when things get rough, companies don't support their employees. It was "everyone for himself and God save the hindermost." In other words, a large group of workers who would quit the minute they found a job elsewhere that provided slightly better wages or working conditions. Job loyalty just didn't exist.

Pleasure in your work (which is different from pleasure at your work) can only happen if free people make the conscious choice to do something together. That is a necessary but not yet a sufficient condition for the motivated employees. They can become motivated, because they are aware and have made a positive choice. Vision and leadership are needed for inspiration to take root and to give it direction.

HAPPINESS AND HAPPY ORGANIZAT

HAPPINESS

and happy organizations

Sparkle!

I think that everyone strives to be happy, although just what that means is not always easy to define. In one of his books, Manfred Kets de Vries, a professor at INSEAD, Europe's leading graduate school of business, in Fontainebleau, recounts an old Chinese saying: "Happiness consists of three things: someone to love, something to do, and something to hope for." Happiness is a difficult phenomenon to describe. For many people it is so difficult that they would rather not think about it. Or they would like to think about it later.

HAPPINESS AND HAPPY ORGANIZ

Striving to reach the goal of happiness is often replaced by striving to reach for wealth, prestige, or power. Exterior manifestations, from which one expects that they will provide a feeling of happiness. But as soon as one attains wealth or power, it is clear that a next step is needed, toward more. Happiness is not determined by success. It does not need wealth or power. The pursuit of these goals is more likely to lead to unhappiness.

And the big question is…

And still there are many organizations where people are rewarded for the pursuit of these forms of so-called happiness. Increased turnover and advances on the career ladder are elements which most organizations (maybe unconsciously) regard as important. You'll never find "being happy" as a goal listed on an evaluation form. Whether or not employees are happy is a question that is never asked. Because that requires defining what is meant by "happiness". I've found — perhaps you have too — that the specious excuse that it's hard to define a certain term is often used to shut off discussion of important questions. But shouldn't it be possible for an organization to ask its employees whether they are happy? Or whether they are happy within the organization in which they work.

Once I conducted an experiment at a company that employed about 1,200 people. At the end of each day the people had to turn off their computers, to log out, as it's called. But the system wouldn't let them log out until they had given a grade for the day. If it had been a great day, they gave it a ten. And if the day had really been very bad, the grade would be a flunking grade. Before this system was introduced, all kinds of human resource employees spent hours discussing how to define a good day. Discussions that led nowhere, as might be expected. Simply asking the question "How do you feel at the end of the day?" seemed too complicated. Still, we persevered. The system of a day evaluation wound up being a resounding success. Every morning on a screen at the entrance of the office you could read the average grade of the day before.

The fluctuations day by day weren't all that significant, but the average line in the grades over the years was interesting indeed. That line rose steadily. Employee satisfaction kept rising. And, at the same time, the profits of the organization also rose. Could there be some connection?

Were the employees of that organization happy after all? Certainly, their feeling of contentment must have been an important factor in the grade that they typed in at the end of every day. At one point, an employee died and there was a collective feeling of sorrow. The grade for that day was very low. But when it was a sunny day, the grade would be somewhat higher. And so you could see how all sorts of events influenced the feelings of employees as revealed in the grades they gave day after day. It would be an exaggeration to claim that these figures indicate a collective feeling of happiness, but they certainly had some bearing on it.

Recently I heard that, generally speaking, young employees have different goals than those belonging to the older generations. While financial independence and security are often high on the agenda among the older ones, a happy life is more important to the younger generation. Or so it seems. That is an important detail if, as manager, you are concerned with the motivation of your team. Take financial independence, for example. The pursuit of wealth is, to many, the same as the pursuit of happiness. Though we all know that as soon as a person has made a lot of money, the pursuit for much more takes over.

The big fish fixation

Or the pursuit of power. A recently appointed CEO told me in response to my asking what his goal was that he wanted to be the best CEO in the world. That would make him very happy. I asked him who at that moment the best CEO was. In other words, whose mirror image would he like to be. It turned out to be Jack Welch, still in his heyday at General Electric. When I mentioned that few people outside the U.S. had ever heard of Jack Welsh, he was staggered. "Why, but everyone knows him," he said. It was clear that, in his eyes, Jack Welch was on a par with God. But enter a supermarket at random and ask people if they've heard of Jack Welch; and people will look at you with blank incomprehension. Not a celebrity. What a blow. The pursuit of an illusion that is supposed to lead to happiness looks to a life in the future instead of life in the present. You often find this among managers, by the way. It's a fast-forward way of looking at things. It's very similar to the old-fashioned rat race. Which does not lead to a stable way of managing.

Pursuing the kind of happiness based on acquiring money and power will frequently encourage others to do likewise. It does not necessarily follow that organizations that strive to become bigger and to make ever-higher profits will provide an environment in which others will find their happiness.

Sparkle!

Misfortune generates energy, too

Let's suppose everyone within an organization strives to be as happy as possible. And every employee has a clear idea of what happiness means for himself or herself. Let's further suppose that, in an extreme case, the goals of the company are not in line with the goals of the employees. Because the way they define happiness is radically different from the way their employers define the word. They're looking for happiness in the present, in their families and children, in feeling rich instead of actually being rich, and in the quality of life. As Kets de Vries says: " People who equate happiness with success (wealth, position and power) will never have enough success to be happy."

Talking about happiness, perhaps you've noticed how often people experience an event that they regard as a disaster at the time, but which they later consider to be the crucial turning point in their life. Being fired, for example, is often experienced as a drama, a blow coming from the angry outside world. This sort of reaction is frequently to be found among those who consider themselves as victims of external circumstances. And who are not capable of creating their own happiness. The accident, the firing, happens to them. I have learned that similar dramas are sometimes a "blessing in disguise", as the saying goes. So they are really little gifts. But they come all wrapped up, concealed, so you don't see them as gifts at the time. Later it often becomes clear that the firing led to a much nicer work environment, a much better bond with your wife and children, or even something totally different. And so a piece of bad luck has contributed to your happiness.

What does that mean?

People are happy when their life has a purpose, if it makes sense. So authentic organizations that strive to give people a sense of meaning provide something that can make them happy. Or with which they can feed their feeling of happiness. Only with giving meaning and significance is happiness possible. The desire of an organization to engage in creative entrepreneurship and to scintillatingly inspire could contribute to the happiness of those who work for the organization. But keep in mind that happy employees, in turn, radiate energy and inspire.

Playing makes people happy. Thus, it follows that creative entrepreneurship combined with sparkling inspiration leads to an environment in which people are happier. An attractive environment to be in. An environment one wants to enter and participate in, as a customer, for example.

We have always been doubtful whether money leads to happiness. But in organizations there is much to be said for the other way around: that happiness leads to money. That's why "the survival of the happiest" is sound doctrine, because those organizations are also "the fittest". The ability to radiate energy and inspire are for the creative entrepreneur at least as important as the bottom line.

BIG
ORGANIZATIONS

Sparkler

CAN ALSO RADIATE

Anyone who has read the preceding chapters might get the feeling that big organizations are cumbersome, slow, dull, sleepy, and uninspiring. Is that the case? Is it really only pleasant, even fun, to work in small, flashy organizations? That would be an exaggeration — an over-general generalization. Of course, there are large organizations in which the atmosphere is terrible and not a single innovative initiative is taken. Where you get the feeling that you are only a tiny cog in a huge machine. And where nobody pays any personal attention to you. But, on the whole, it's not for nothing that large organizations have become as large as they are. And mostly they stay large and keep on growing on the basis of capable people and good products and services — and care for their people...

Recently I spoke with a customer of a large privatized, formerly state-owned company. He started out by running down the management of the company, and going on at some length. The company had no interest in its customers. It stifled entrepreneurial spirit. Everything was all very badly managed. But after venting for a while, he agreed that, yes, there must be some capable managers because the company was doing well. There are various opinions about large organizations — both bad and good. It all depends on who you ask. If you ask a successful entrepreneur who's been starting and making companies grow all his life, you're likely to hear a lot of talk about red tape and bureaucracy. But if you ask that same entrepreneur about his own worries, you'll hear stories about eighty-hour workweeks and cash flow problems. Small entrepreneurial companies really have just as many disadvantages as large companies. Nothing is ever right...

Grandfather said...

Ever since I was a boy I wanted to have my own company. It all started when I went to the United States for a year after finishing high school. In that far-away country that desire was strengthened. My grandfather, for whom I always had a lot of respect, had owned his own business all his life. So I was really astonished when, after I got my masters in business economics, he strongly urged me to find a job at a multinational, like Philips. I would have a good life, a secure life, and more fun than working for some small firm. And, in fact, I did get a job with Philips. But, as I say, at the time, his advice really amazed me. How was it possible that a dyed-in-the-wool entrepreneur like my grandfather would advise others that it was better not to be your own boss.

Later, after I had started and sold my first company, I understood what he was telling me. The constant worries, the constant work pressure that comes with owning and running one's own company can be exhausting. The whole business of being an entrepreneur can be a hoot, very amusing, even addictive. Sometimes so addictive that you can't think of anything else but your company twenty-four hours per day. Seven days a week, day in day out. And that can be very wearing and off-putting for your partner and your kids. And if you're not careful, you will lose them after a while. Because it is very difficult to figure out how to achieve the right balance between the work involved in owning your own company and the time and effort involved in sustaining a relationship. Whether your own company is large or small makes no difference.

On the other hand, take a really large firm, a company like Shell, Philips, General Motors. What's so different about them? Don't their employees work and have to worry just as much about maintaining a balance in their lives? Of course, they do. But being part of a large organization is very different from being the owner of one. The feeling must be very different for Michael Dell of Dell Computers, for example, to lead his company than for the top manager of an energy company. For the one, the company is his own, his life's work; for the other, it's a job. Which doesn't mean that one is doing his job better than the other. But one is an entrepreneur and the other a top manager. I'm convinced that if a large company wants to grow and wants to be a pleasant place to work for, it must have an entrepreneurial top manager. Managers who are solely concerned with making money and following routine business practices and who boost profits by cutting down on turnover will, in the long run, prove to be a disaster for every organization.

At around the turn of the last century — from around 1992 until 2002

— there was a true boom of new companies. Venture capital appeared from everywhere, and initiatives were popping up one after another. And what a party it was! Unbelievable. Which is not exactly what I have in mind when I'm talking about fun. Having fun and partying are, to my thinking, not synonymous. The association with parties is hard to break, but fun is getting pleasure from your work. And getting pleasure from your work does not come from parties. It has to do with contentment, with colleagues, with the work environment, with making a profit, with the flow you find yourself in. Fun is the most important element. Because if someone gets pleasure from his or her work, the work will go smoothly, by itself. And usually the results are also good. Because if the results aren't good, you usually won't get that much pleasure from your work. Why is that? Because results, including financial results, are a part of the fun.

I can still see them, the so-called entrepreneurs of the dot.com boom, who with other people's money, were going to town everywhere. For that matter, the investors, the shareholders were just as culpable as the managers themselves. Because the money was being pumped at an enormous pace into new start-ups. At the same time, less and less attention was paid to the quality of the business plans. And was that fun? Very soon, it became clear that the golden rule of making a profit in the long term was still valid. And so the companies that ran through their money had to search desperately for actual, real-life customers. For real money and not for money borrowed from the shareholders. The lesson learned was that it was no fun at all to spend a lot of money very fast to pay for beautiful advertising campaigns and lavish parties. It wasn't fun, it was frustrating. The start-ups that survived that giddy period are having fun. The value of their stocks has risen since those days, and making a profit is now fun.

Not a question of scale

In the meantime, it has become clear that fun is not so much related to the size of an organization as it is to its culture, and, more specifically, with the atmosphere created by the leader. Pleasure in your work is the energy source that's needed. One employee will feel comfortable in a large organization, another will feel lost in it. Some feel at home in a large company, others will find it depressing. They don't want to be a number. But if someone feels like a number in an organization, then clearly that organization works with numbers. Instead of with people. And yet we should not forget that, when it comes to finding pleasure in your work, you yourself are responsible, not the organization. You yourself are always responsible for your own pleasure, I cannot emphasize this enough. Because if the place, the environment, the management, is not to your

Sparkle!

liking, you take steps. For example, you can make it pleasurable or you can work somewhere else. You set your own goals.

Getting back to the question of whether large corporations can also be fun, you have to take a look at yourself. What do you want? What is important to you in your life? What is it that makes your life fun and worth living? There lies the beginning of the answer to the question. And only when you've answered that question can you start to move toward finding the place that's right for you — working with a small group of ten colleagues or with a giant multinational. Granted, it's harder to have a clear idea of all the elements that determine the level of fun within an organization that employs tens of thousands, but it can be done. It is possible to avoid getting caught in constricting bureaucratic rules. Rules that destroy individualism and that kill people. But there again the responsibility ultimately lies with the individual. Take a close look at yourself. How did you adapt to the corporate culture, the rules of the organization for which you work? Did you remain critical or did you just adapt and slog on, no longer keeping your dreams and ambitions in mind as something to strive for? Because that can happen, and, before you know it, you're caught up in the circus of meetings that often are about nothing anymore. Or they could be all wrapped up in five minutes. Leaving time for having fun, for doing things that are useful.

Don't hide your feelings

When I headed the international IT company Origin, I was often struck by the disproportionate part of my time that was spent, or lost, on meetings that didn't contribute very much to the business or to the company. So you wind up spending all those hours before you can actually settle down and do the real work. And is that fun? Does that get you into a flow? Absolutely not. It drains the energy out of your body. At a place where you find work and colleagues that stimulate you and are fun to be with, good results generate energy; the wrong work environment leave you feeling burned out. You felt it immediately, at least if you pay attention. Because burn-out and being overworked, often the result of having the energy drained out of you for years, is something you could have foreseen. Pay attention! Are you having fun — or none at all? If you're not having fun, don't hide that feeling. Do something about it.

Big corporations can after all be fun. They can pay attention to people, they can be result-oriented, and they can be stimulating. At smaller organizations it is somewhat easier to provide direction and improve conditions than at large corporations. But both can provide it. The fun.

Time and again I come across large rather stolid or conservative companies at which, all of a sudden, there's a surprising surge of creativity. Often it seems as if such creativity is almost out of place there – an anomaly – but on closer examination you find that these initiatives were frequently set in motion by a few colleagues. That's what I call fun, when an organization doesn't stifle initiatives, but lets them blossom.

Sparkle!

Survival
of the Happiest

Sparkle!

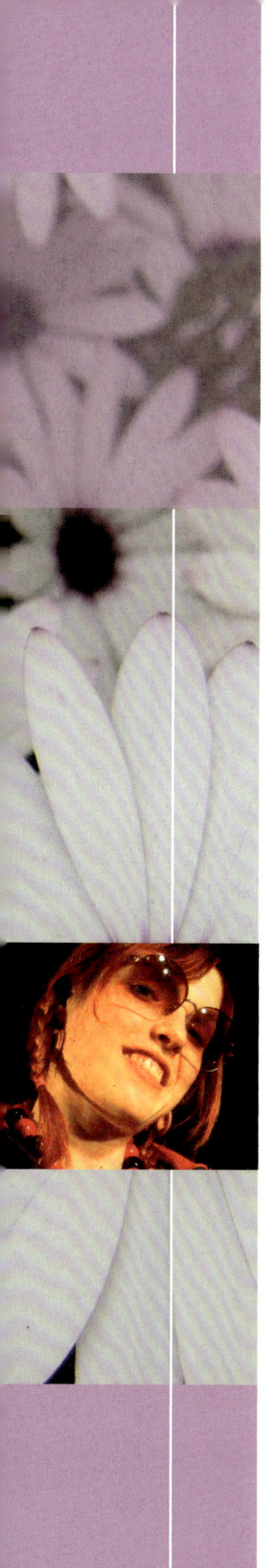

Happy Campers

In the same way that Darwin spoke of the survival of the fittest in Origin of Species, nowadays there's talk within organizations of the survival of the happiest. Why must words like "fun," "playing," "creativity," and "happiness" always be followed by the remark, "Well, but doesn't it all boil down to the bottom line?" Time and again I've seen how much play and enjoyment are appreciated in the workplace, but in the next breath people will come up with some Calvinist comment about money. Does an organization that is motivated, happy, fun to be a part of automatically turn a profit, make money? No, but an organization where there is no fun to be had isn't worth keeping afloat.

People spend a substantial part of their lives at work. At their work, as they say. And, as I see it, that work has to be worthwhile. It has to provide almost as much pleasure as the things people spend their time doing off the job. So it's a good sign if an organization and its manager put a premium on the pleasure their employees get while on the job. It is at least as important as holding all those meetings about key performance indicators.

Customers are to some extent involved with the employees of the company. Now imagine that those employees are to some degree free to be themselves, to make themselves comfortable in their own skin. If they feel comfortable in their own skin, their customers will also feel comfortable. If they seem glum, that's the impression they'll make on the customer, who won't be motivated to keep up the relationship. Everywhere these days the customer is number one. What customer wants to deal with an unmotivated, uninterested, and unhappy employee? After all, customers are only human.

Well, truly happy

And that's only one aspect of the crucial importance of having employees who are truly happy campers. Because those same employees also influence their colleagues. Who, in

What customer wants to deal with an unmotivated, uninterested, and unhappy employee?

return, respond just like their customers. It doesn't get us anywhere when we get each other down. A financial manager once said to me: "But we don't want a company full of happy campers." People laughed because it did sound funny when he put it that way. But the fact is, that's exactly what we do want — an organization in which all the employees are genuinely happy campers. Because people respond to that. They love happy campers. And, if we're honest, deep down don't we want to be happy campers ourselves? Because the alternative is not very appealing — the serious, sober guy who never cracks a joke. That's the road that leads to burn-out.

Survival of the happiest means that no person can function day in and day out, year after year in an environment where pleasure is not the central focus point. Where the main concern is not that the employees enjoy their work. Naturally, that does not have to happen each moment in every day. Everyone knows that life, which includes one's job, has its ups and downs. And that goes for every level in the organization. It is a mistake to suppose that the pursuit of a pleasurable, motivating environment is reserved only for managers. I have encountered many employees — entry level and up — who made a party of their tasks. They wanted to be the best or the most amusing or the most charming and most friendly whatever — elevator man, receptionist, or mailroom wallah. And they themselves got enormous pleasure from that. How do I know this? Because everyone is talking about it and these so-called happy camper employees have a tremendous impact on their organization. Everyone knows them, because everyone likes them.

And now the fun starts

But if you're in a management position and you don't pay attention to the fact that the survival of the happiest is an essential success factor for every organization, you might forget it. Because it does take time. And… money. Yes, because to give people the feeling that you care about them and that they are permitted to be happy requires spending a lot of time and money.

I started up a large reorganization once. The employees were told to assemble in the cafeteria where the reorganization was announced. The mood was generally depressed, with reactions like "This will be about the umpteenth reorganization," even though the whole point of the reorganization was to revitalize the company, boost morale. The conclusion was that people just don't believe it, or have stopped believing, that things would improve. Try it yourself sometime: as manager, tell your employees that, from now on, things are going to be really fun. Was it not any fun before? People just don't believe it. You have to deliver proof fast.

In the reorganization mentioned above, we started with three simple matters: everyone would get wall-to-wall carpeting instead of depressing linoleum, all the rooms would be freshly painted, and every employee would get a new PC. The message we wanted to get across was that we wanted to improve the work environment of each and every employee, to make it more pleasant. It did the trick. In reorganizations it's often forgotten that displays, new organization schemes, number of employees, and so on have little or no direct impact on the work environment. By physically showing that one cares for each individual employee, the belief in other changes increased dramatically, and the results improved more rapidly than anyone could have expected. The reorganization quickly became a big success, and the projected increase in profit margins was reached within the first year. Incidentally the slogan we came up with for this reorganization, was actually the word FUN. At first it was regarded with a little suspicion but it was finally truly experienced .

Hands off the fun

If it's about increasing profits, the first thing a manager will think of doing is applying cost-cutting strategies. Because that's the easiest thing to do. And you will always see, that when they start cutting costs, the first to go are all those things that have to do with fun. Because cutting back is not fun! Or, if there are layoffs, we won't be able to have any more fun. That's the atmosphere unfortunately associated with cutbacks. Having fun is no longer permitted. This, despite the fact that it has played a crucial part in boosting productivity! And do the happiest campers survive the cutbacks? Well, no. The talents just leave the tent, because they'll be looking for an environment they can thrive in. So you've lost those. And the employees who cannot leave that easily will keep on plugging, but not with a lot of pleasure. And thus with a drop in productivity.

Happy campers, to continue using the honorific title, are the sparkplugs of any organization. Preferably you would have a lot of them. But you've got to cherish them, because they tend to be critical of their environment. And don't forget, happy campers cost money! But the good news is that they bring in much more revenue. So you dare yourself to become a happy camper. Because even a manager can be one.

The House

of Fun

I want to emphasize that talking about a problem, and keeping the conversation going, will go a long way toward solving it. Talking about the difficulty of solving it, that is. Because even if you don't yet know the solution, bringing the difficulties to the fore is already a big step in the right direction. So, if you want to have a dynamic company, keep telling each other, reminding each other that that's your goal. And, above all, if you want to succeed with your customers, you have to tell each other, too. If you want to have happy and motivated employees, you must let them know this, too. Is that the solution? No, of course not, but it's a big step in the right direction.

Sparkle!

IN DEEPEST SECRECY, WE HAD SOMEONE PAINT IN GIANT LETT. ABOVE THE ENTRANCE: HOUSE OF FUN.

Are we still a little proud?

After I was asked to go ahead with the reorganization designed to return a large data center to profitability, I had to deal with those cultural differences. How do you make the company proud and dynamic again? That was the question. My answer: by talking about it a lot. By coming up with an offbeat slogan: "It's Fun@......". By being very specific about what we wanted, we quickly found that the company was moving in the right direction. Simply by stating the desired objective we achieved very soon that the company was moving into the right direction. Furthermore, we paired the slogan with a number of very visible deeds, like complete renovation of the total office environment. The wished-for uptick in profitability soon followed.

To clarify the objective. How do you do that? By naming it, by continually communicating it with others, by linking it with visible actions. Three very important steps. You have to take all three. That last element — linking it with concrete actions — is the one that is usually left out. It costs money and in a period in which the focus is on result-based improvements, it often seems the wrong tack to take. But people want more than just words. They want the sense that things are really changing. They want to see and experience something physically. Which, in turn, immediately motivates a group to get a move on, to do big things.

I recall the time when I had to oversee a merger between two somewhat smaller IT companies. Both companies were involved with a rather advanced technology. Both employed a good bunch of young people, but they never worked together on anything. And now they had to get together. To start with, we selected a building in which they would all have to fit. That would seem to be only logical, but a lot of mergers are nothing more than financial engineering actions. So the merger looks like a merger but there is no real change in culture. To shareholders, the merged company may look as if it is bigger and better, but if you check out the numbers to see what is really happening, you'll see that it's all much ado about nothing. There are quite a few companies quoted on the stock exchange whose mergers mean nothing more than gluing the businesses together financially. With a value for stockholders, but only a financial one. That is often enough, but you don't create real companies that way.

Okay, then. The merger. Enthusiastic people, but two cultures. Putting them together in one building, in an old building, built in the seventies — as dull as dishwater. It would be a bummer. In deepest secrecy, we painted above the entrance in giant letters HOUSE OF FUN. We wanted to strike the right note from day one. It had to make a splash. It had to be the most dynamic and especially the most fun company in San Francisco. Inside, too, we had secretly done something with the colors of the decor. And it worked, it was the talk of the town. What fun! Who was doing something like that? On the street, too, people spoke about it. I will never forget that a subtenant of the building, an insurance agent, put me immediately on the spot. It was a bloody shame to call the building the House of Fun. The agency he worked for was a serious business. What would their customers think? He wanted the offending words removed right away. No delay. That discussion was a great boon to us, especially when we went public with it.

Sparkle!

ENJOYING,

Sparkle!

NOT SO EASY!

Sparkle!

I'm not a great fan of getting up early in the morning. In the days when I drove 50,000 miles a year with a driver, I asked my driver to show up at my door at 7:00 a.m. As a means of encouraging me to get up early. It helped, because I pitied him having to stand around waiting for me to get out of bed.

Blissing out

At that time I was the CEO of a very large company. Worked day and night and often through the weekend. Until one day a colleague said to me, "You have to learn to enjoy." Whah? Learn to enjoy? Or did he say, "Are you enjoying it enough?" A good question: do we enjoy the things that are all around us enough? While I was working hard to finish this book, I often sat in my workroom in France. Bent over while typing and from time to time leaning back in the chair to contemplate the text. But far too seldom did I look out of the window. Because out there lay the true treasure. A view over several valleys and hills, beautiful scenery that unfurled in front of me in several different layers. Here and there a ribbon of mist, smoke twisting from a chimney. For hours you could look at it. Enjoying the peace and quiet that radiated from that landscape. If only I had not been so busy typing this book!

Enjoying what you have, whatever that may be. Whether it is a seashell, a view, a child, a flower, a house, or whatever it is. Just enjoying is so very difficult. It takes time to let the impressions penetrate. It takes time to enjoy something. And we don't often give ourselves that time. Not long ago I heard a beautiful story that illustrates this very point — and it's a true story, by the way. A top manager of a large American company announced to his team that he was now working "his very hardest." Hm. Let's hope you see the humor in this.

How can you possibly think that you are working hard, then even harder, and then your very hardest. What is that? Is that a feeling that you are giving it your all? Does it ever occur to you that maybe there's a different way to get the job done? That it's got to be done differently? That by working less hard you might actually accomplish more. That by enjoying the small things in life you will start to think much more positively, so that suddenly things will start to happen on their own? Of course, in Holland and many other countries there is a so-called Protestant work ethic: enjoying your work is not allowed. Enjoying your children and your home life, your private life, is allowed. But enjoying your work? Sitting still for a moment, looking around, absorbing what's going on around you, that does take time, a lot of time. We are inclined to postpone enjoying for a while. Later, after hours, then I'll really enjoy my old sports car. Yes, later, in due course I will really enjoy my house in Italy. Soon I will really start to enjoy my grandchildren, to make up for too often having forgotten to pay attention to my children. In the future my wife and I are going to do a lot of fun things I don't have time for now. Yes, it's all going to happen later. It is going to be a busy time....later.

Have you had enough fun?
Imagine that in the personal evaluations of employees there would be a section dealing with how much the employee had enjoyed working in your company. Imagine that at the evaluation interview, your manager said, "You've performed very well, but, unfortunately, because you have not sufficiently enjoyed your work, you won't get a bonus." How does that sound — illogical, right? Because you would enjoy receiving a bonus. But that financial reward is really of much less value than the kind of enjoyment we're talking about here. Enjoying life, the present, the people around you. Not that stupid amount of money. Come on. Stop it already.

Something serious has to happen before people realize all the things they could and should enjoy. First one needs a signal from the outside, which penetrates and gets under your skin. Someone dies — some elderly acquaintance or a loved one. Or a child falls seriously ill. Why is it that people can't just learn on their own — without this kind of shock — what enjoyment is? Sometimes you see companies that are led by leaders full of energy who do everything right. But they haven't learned how to enjoy yet. They work like horses, they are intelligent, sometimes amusing. But the sense of perspective does not exist, or not yet. Lost souls, I call them sometimes. You can see that they haven't lived much. And for those who believe in previous lives, you could say that these lost souls have had no previous lives, or only a few. They are young. Haven't lived through really rough times. I recently saw a cute young girl, five years old. If you looked closely, you could see right off that she was an old soul. She had inherited the wisdom of her ancestors. I thought I recognized a few people. Young souls are willing, but they don't have the knowledge yet. And they haven't yet discovered that enjoying is the most important thing in life.

Enjoying your work in a company. Taking that with you in an evaluation interview. Assigning a value to it. To acknowledge its importance. Explicitly stating that this is important. Is enjoying yourself the same as fun? No, not really, I think. As Matt Weinstein writes in Managing to Have Fun: "Work is not supposed to be fun, that's why it's called work." To create an environment in which it is fun to work is decidedly different from enjoying. Although they do have something to do with each other.

Where can you find enjoyment at and during your work? Let's start with enjoying a small success. Is that what usually happens? Well, no. Success is just taken to be the norm. In my present company we've come up with the term we use when we score a deal or succeed in some other way. We call it scoring a Yippee. Anyone who has a Yippee to report is allowed to report it to one and all at any moment. It is even mandatory. Before we just scored orders, had satisfied customers (sometimes less than satisfied, by the way), or we had a fun day. That was never shared with others. Why not? I think just because we didn't pay attention to this matter. Most companies accept successes as a matter of course. But sharing is essen-

Sparkle!

tial. You can't talk enough about it. Or should we only share problems with each other? Because that's often the case these days. Now we have something horrible like e-mail, with which we can bother each other at any moment and share trouble. Particularly just before the weekend.

Fresh start for the week

Another rule I have imposed is that on Friday afternoon, a time when nobody can change the situation, you are never allowed to bother someone else with a problem message or a problem e-mail. You would send the other person into the weekend under a cloud of negativity. Thanks a lot! Or a SMS (Short Message Service), where you leave a nasty message. Easy, because the other party can't immediately respond. No, in that respect e-mail and SMS's are emotionally charged means of communication, if you don't know how to handle them. Extremely effective for putting a big dent in the enjoyment.

Enjoying a weekend will give a lot of energy, and you'll be able to start the new week fresh. Ruining the enjoyment drains off the energy. Imagine, you are driving home on Friday afternoon with the sun shining and you receive a SMS at the last moment, in which an employee shares the news of a Yippee — a beautiful deal that was just signed. Whistling and happy, the weekend gets off to a great start. That's how it should be. That's what we have to aim for and pay attention to. Those small things make such a big difference. But all too often it seems that these simple things are too little to apply to an office situation, too insignificant to notice. Just like that flower, or that smiling child. Enjoying is in the details. They can't be noticed if they aren't there, but make a difference if they are.

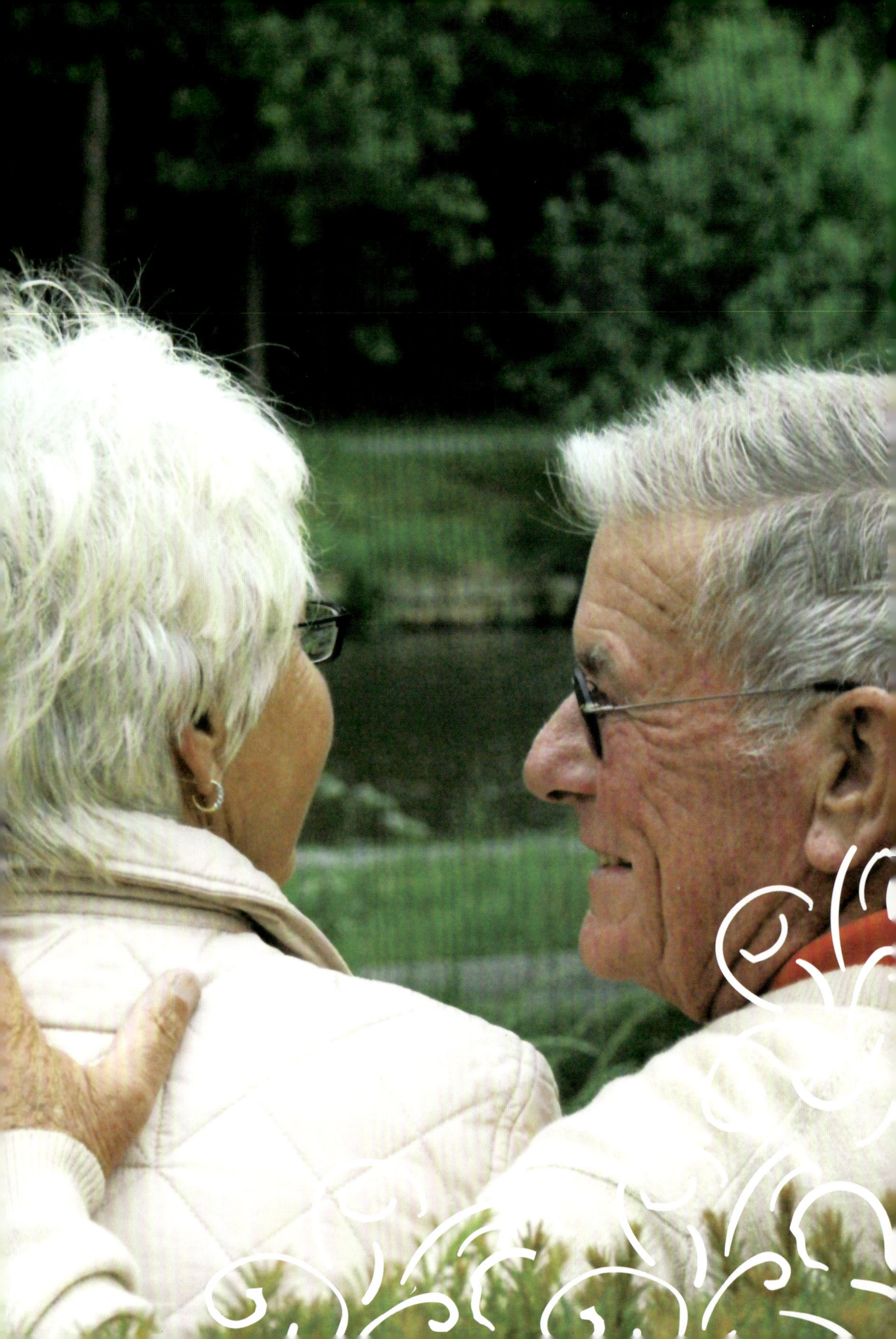

Sparkling and touching

To get tears in your eyes. Listening or looking With a lump in your throat. You are moved, touched. You can be overcome with emotion at many moments and in many places. But it is always special. And in a sense, beautiful.

Take sparkling. Things that sparkle cheer you, make you happy. It gives things a yellow or blue tint, and it's fresh, refreshing. Sparkling energizes. Radiating. Tingling. Sparkling is also a word that makes you happy. How often, in our companies or organizations, are we emotionally touched, moved? How often do they sparkle? Most organizations, sad to say, never or only rarely offer such an experience. An organization that sparkles. What are we talking about, anyway? We can say that a theater company sparkles from time to time. A wonderful play that makes the audience happy. Or a soccer team that wins the game with a sparkling, last-minute goal.

But a really sparkling company, or big organization of any kind? Can you name even one truly sparkling, scintillating company? Well, yes, there are some that would put themselves in that category, but what matters most is whether the company scintillates in the eyes of its customers, of the market. The customer has to be convinced that it is fun to do business with a certain organization. Throughout the world, Apple is thought of as a truly scintillating organization. Offering products that stimulate, products that sparkle. They are more expensive than comparable products, yes, but even so, people go for them. When Apple came out with the new iPod, there were already quite a few MP3 players on the market.

Sparkle!

Moreover, the product Apple brought out was more expensive than most others. And still millions of people switched and bought this expensive product. Why? The answer is obvious: because both the company and the product sparkle. As consumer you want to be part of that. Part of the sparkling.

The sparkling garbage man

How many sparkling companies can you think of? Give yourself time to think about this and let all those sparkling companies flow through your mind. You will notice that small companies sparkle sooner than big ones. If their employees sparkle, so will the company. You'll be eager to do business with them. And, by the way, you'll see individuals within corporations who stand out because they sparkle. A mail clerk, a garbage man, a manager, you'll know who they are. Their presence can give the company that employs them a sparkling image. Then, suddenly you notice that there are tens of thousands of sparkling people. That gives hope. Why do we go to the one restaurant and not the other? Because at that one restaurant there is a chef or a maitre'd we like a lot — a person who sparkles.

But sparkling organizations, no, you don't see them that often. Many organizations appeal to the market through clever marketing campaigns full of glitzy images. But when the market senses that the message doesn't ring true, the company loses points instead of gaining customers. The image is dulled, not brightened. Moreover, the company loses credit with the public. It winds up looking pathetic, a company that has tried to deceive you. The market does not believe the message if it does not agree with how you feel about it. There are companies that think they can make themselves appear sparkling simply by promoting that image in an ad campaign. They'll spend millions of dollars on the campaign — and that's where it will end. As soon as the customers have to deal with the company they'll notice that, despite all the fancy ads, the atmosphere is the same. Nothing has changed. The people with whom they are dealing are still just as boring as before. In short, the campaign has flopped. How about spending all that money on really changing the company? But there are still advertising agencies that believe that the first priority should be to develop the campaign and only then to change the company itself. If those changes are ever really made.

Being moved, touched. Many things can do this to us. The sight of a beautiful flower, the light on the water, a beautiful story, a small child who is crying, a dreadful situation in a war zone. It comes on you suddenly, the emotion. It wells up. You don't think, now I am going to be moved by something. I myself am moved by the most absurd situations in a movie. The tears are streaming down my face. But are there any companies or organizations that move me to tears? No, I couldn't name any off the top of my head. But there are numerous situations that take place in organizations that are touching. A colleague who is saying farewell, a thank-you, a group of employees who have composed a song for a colleague who is ill…

A product that stirs emotion

Stirring and sparkling. It is always the people who do it. The environment, the organization, the company where they work, stimulates it. Or it does not stimulate. There are chilling environments where sparkling is not seen as useful. Where people really think that it is all about earning money, turning a profit. Everyone agrees, wholeheartedly, that this sissy stuff is all just nonsense. Forget about sparkling, get over it. To inspire customers, what's that all about? Forget it. The fact that almost all customers appreciate sparkling products is easily overlooked when we put on our efficiency glasses. We don't even notice it.

Others have written about this before: touching customers, touching the market, by sparkling and motivating. And that goes for almost all products. Especially for the products that are indistinguishable from other products. The mass-market products that we call the "commodities." But it is precisely with those products that it's essential to add some sparkle. Because it certainly does make a difference which salesperson is trying to sell us a cell phone. If the salesperson has a sense of humor, is pleasant, and sparkles, he or she can easily ask a little more for the product and anyhow will sell more. If the organization that salesperson works for agrees, this kind of behavior will be encouraged, stimulated. Or not, and a normal dull salesperson will be in the shop.

It is essential that a company stimulates and that there's a sense of sparkle in the air, of an emotional charge. That this is considered important. Why? First of all, because it's human, the way we work. Secondly, it's fun. And third, it will pay off for the organization. The company will no longer be the chilling environment in which we earn our salary out of need, where in the morning we fight our way through traffic jams to get to our office, and then spend the rest of the day yawning behind our desks. Sparkling and stirring emotion — the lifeblood of every organization. Without which the company is dead. And nobody wants anything to do with them, neither employees nor customers.

Sparkle!

An entertaining

sparkle!

dinnerparty, sir

During a brainstorming session for setting up a training program, we were discussing the elements needed to actually come in contact with a customer. Which is not that easy. For some people, it's just second nature. They regard it the same as coming in contact with any other human being. But my own feeling is that, for most people, it's a challenge.

To make emotional contact with your customer, to kindle some emotion, to provide an incentive — inspire. That's what it's all about. A mass promotion, for example, with baseball caps or free pens. But also for small groups of business customers. You can stir the emotions of a large group of people by telling them a story that catches their attention. The way Ralph Lauren does with the story about style and the way Marlboro did it the story of the tough cowboy. All such narratives are designed to touch people, form a connection. Are meant to make a company that's lagging in the market into something more than just a shirt or a cigarette. Involving the emotions of the customer will enhance loyalty because the customer wants to stay tuned. In his entertaining book The Dream Society: How the Coming Shift from Information to Imagination Will Transform Your Business, Rolf Jensen writes that a company has no right to exist if it can't come up with a narrative that extends into the future. And he has a point. Because no company can survive if all it does is produce beautiful products for the lowest price. Selling commodities at bargain prices to customers who are not loyal is a lost cause. Because they too want to

Sparkle!

hear a story, and they want to belong to something. And that makes it suddenly much simpler…stirring emotion with stories.

Granting = friends

But how would you get this going with a new business customer, for example? How do you enter into a relationship like that? It is clear that's what is needed. A customer would much rather have business deals with someone he likes and with someone he knows well than with an unfriendly stranger. In any case, the product alone isn't enough. Above and beyond superior products and service, there remains the need to build a relationship in the business market. I would even go so far as to say that, despite all the rules relating to bidding for contracts, personal relationships account for more than 50 percent of the deals that are made. This is sometimes called granting. For some reason — basically, to avoid fraud and personal enrichment — all kinds of procedures have been devised to turn the purchasing process into a circus. When years ago I announced to my board of directors that I had awarded a project to two suppliers, their first reaction was surprise — those suppliers were friends of mine! Was that kosher? Was it ethical? Had I acted in compliance with contract law? My response to that was that they were friends and that is exactly why they got the order. I trusted them and I knew their way of operating through and through. And that is the reason they got the order. Furthermore, by awarding the contracts to them we would avoid months of looking at bids and other contracting procedures.

But still the logic of this reasoning was murky. Have we lost something along the way? Is there a desire at work here to make the purchase and sales process completely objective? If that were to happen, a process that, above all else, has to do with instinct, with one's gut reaction, would lose all of its passion. Because whether millions of consumers are involved or a single business customer, the process is always associated with the stirring of emotion.

Prick your own fork

Personally, I can communicate best with a customer if I am face to face with him. When we can see eye to eye. When I can see what the reaction is. Instead of writing letters or e-mails, or instead of asking my secretary to call. The latter is, of course, often an admission of weakness. Important business connections you always call yourself. That obviously will be appreciated more than the other way of getting in touch. I noticed that this practice is more common in the United States than the rest of the world. But it still leaves a kind of distance that may have something to do with status. The real contact, eye contact, is best made during a dinner. I dine a lot with my clients! And, besides, those dinners have to be enjoyable. Otherwise you might as well eat at home. Dress-up dinner functions are something else again; you should try to attend as few as possible. They are only a waste of time. A dinner invitation is something you should take care of yourself. It has to be something special. Eating together at a restaurant chosen with great care. Because your choice signals the respect you have for your business relation. If you want to impress a woman, you don't take her to MacDonald's, do you?

A nice dinner, sir. Truly cordial, good fun. Good wine. Nothing done in haste. Pay attention to details. Personal attention. And discuss matters that really count. A very nice book has been written on this subject: The World Café, Shaping Our Futures through Conversations that Matter. Because at such a carefully arranged dinner with a customer who is important to you, the discussion has to lead somewhere. The best way is not to talk about business during the whole dinner. Does that sound strange? Not a word about work? Isn't that a waste of time? Are you crazy, carrying on a conversation with a possible client without talking about business when you could be spending the time with loved ones? You've got to talk about something. About important business. Like, for example, the question "How are you?" but then not just casually, but sincerely, wanting an honest answer. How does someone feel in his or her work? What are your hobbies?

Talking about the matters that truly preoccupy people is that what they would like to talk about but aren't used to doing in a work environment. In The World Café, notes are scribbled on the tablecloth, but most good restaurants don't encourage that sort of thing, nor would they appreciate it. Although it wouldn't be that crazy an idea to bring your own damask tablecloth, and some good felt-tip markers, and write during the meal. Quite creative really, and also startling. But do take care to let the restaurant owner in on your plans beforehand. That tablecloth, written full of notes of things discussed that evening, things that really matter — what do you do with it? You can give it to your prospective client to take along as a reminder of an evening well spent. I have to admit, I've never done that, but I will — and soon. Your business relation will show it to the wife and kids at home and he won't be in a hurry to wash it. Speaking about sealing a bond!

Strange table conversation
One day I had dinner with an important customer and I knew that during that evening I had to talk business for a moment, because I wanted to secure the order for the coming year. I was somewhat tense about it, be-

cause for us it would be an important order. And still I did not know how and when I should start to talk about it. The dinner was very cozy and was getting to the end. At a certain moment I decided to go about it totally differently. Behave a little crazy: "I have been thinking about the order that we may be carrying out for you next year. It's so important that we have decided to take it on. We will complete the order whether you pay or not. It's just too important to stop now." There, I had said it. I raised my glass and proposed a toast. The customer was perplexed. Uncertain and half-laughing, he asked me if he wasn't the one who should have said this. "Isn't it usually the customer who gives the order," he said, "or am I wrong? But I agree with you, the order is too important for us, so we will continue. And we do want to pay for it too."

That was a strange conversation, but it was also a lot of fun. So bizarre or maybe comical that neither of us will soon forget it. Try that sometime in an office environment. In an office, sitting behind desks, both of you in uniform, with your neckties on. Such a conversation could never have taken place in an environment like that. But the magic of a place, the magic of an emotional connection made during a good dinner makes everything possible. It creates friendship, it creates a bond. During a good dinner you can do anything. Try it yourself.

139

Inspire

Four professionals had a dream

How important can it be to inspire? To inspire the customer, inspire your employees, and inspire yourself. To be uninspired is certainly a reason for failure. To be unable to inspire your customers means being unable to catch their interest, fascinate them. Every one enjoys being inspired, to be touched, moved. One of the most inspiring companies I know is called Made in Scotland. But that is not totally by accident...

Years ago four golf professionals decided to work together. Why? Because they had become friends over the years. Two Scots, an American, and a Dutchman. And keep in mind the fact that, as a rule, golf professionals like to run their businesses by themselves and have hardly any experience in working together. Golf is a sport in which you are mostly on your own. You can hardly describe it as a team sport. The four professionals all had years of golf experience under their belts. They knew of nothing else but golf. Golf governed their lives completely. So to take on a project that required collaboration with others, that was a very different story.

The creation of a company

Even so, some kind of business had developed with the four friends. They took customers along to foreign countries where they played golf together. And in this way, over the years, they had built up an impressive list of customers. But they didn't use that list. Then, some while ago, after another successful golf event in Scotland, the four men sat, a little drunk perhaps, in a castle in front of the open fireplace daydreaming. They began to share with each other their dreams. Dreams of a fabulous company that would make it possible for them— and their customers — to participate in the best and most beautiful golf tournaments imaginable.

And there, at that point in the dreams, the company Made in Scotland was created. Made in Scotland. And their mission statement: "Four professionals had a dream. To create their own unique golf team. Committed to your improvement, quality, and fun. Inspired by their pure love of the Game. They bring their plan into action. This idea was Made in Scotland." This dream is important — and inspiring as well. Take a look what it says. Love for the sport. A commitment to quality, to improvement. To have the desire to do everything you do to the best of your ability. To always deliver the highest quality. All those things inspire the world.

And with that dream a beginning had to be made. These golf professionals, like most other people, didn't know much about starting a company. And so that element had to be added to the dream. In the following years they searched for a beginning. Because how do you go about realizing that dream? First and foremost: hold on to it and never water down the wine. In the beginning of 2000 I met the four men during such a golf event in Scotland with my customers. And after that successful event, I offered to put aside some time one evening to help them set up a company. Because just as they had their dreams, it had always been my dream to create companies. It turned out to be a good combination, because after that first evening of talking about what steps you have to take to set up a company, many more evenings followed. And after those many evenings, a plan evolved. And the plan turned into a company. A company that employs around twenty people and that is affiliated with some seventy companies. Did that just happen like one, two, three? Yes looking back five years and thinking about it, it did happen one, two, three. At least, that's how it feels. Of course, it didn't happen all by itself. But the tireless energy the four founders put into it inspired customer after customer to join in.

Customer plays golf well

For me the first five years after establishing the company were as much a learning process as it was for the four golf pros. Because every time I had to explain to them exactly how you go about the project businesswise, I discovered that that wasn't what it's all about. Yes, it is essential that you set up a company on a sound footing. That there be a sound administration, that everything is set down in accordance with the law, and that the services offered have been thought through with the greatest care. And so on. Because just as a large corporation that has to have its plans and projections all carefully prepared, the same goes for a small company. But what I learned was how much fun it is to work in a company where everything is done with love and care. Where nothing else is as important as the customer. Because Made in Scotland was brought into being by people who always put themselves last when it comes to customers. The customer always has priority, is always right, and is always a good golfer. And you rarely come across that attitude. Sometimes you see this level of customer contact in restaurants or hotels, because there, too, the customer should be the central focus and the employees are trained to always be courteous, attentive to the needs of the customer. Even so, it has to be in your genes. That's why one restaurant or hotel is better than another. In some hotels they are pleasant and attentive because that's the rule, as it should be. But the point is that they are courteous and attentive to your needs because it gives them pleasure. And that is the secret. To deal with a customer in a pleasant way, because it gives you pleasure, and not because that's the way it should be. You have it in you, or you don't. And the customer notices this right away. What a super feeling it must be for a customer to notice that the pleasant way he or she is being dealt with comes from the heart.

It could be better

Speaking about golf. Is the game really a sport? Whether it is or not, one thing is certain: it is extremely challenging and sometimes you wind up fighting against yourself. Because the harder you try to improve your game, the worse it gets. But not necessarily. You ought to try to go onto the golf course with one of Made in Scotland professionals. I've often had the experience of playing with someone who could not play the game at all, who could not hit one ball right. It can put you in a pretty bad mood. But not the guys of Made in Scotland. They see something good in every bad swing or shot. Very slowly and painstakingly, they coach the duffer to make miniscule improvements. Improvements that seem so small that they are a magical touch. Because here lies a secret as well. Everyone who has played golf at some point knows that the application of improvements at any one time often leads to a worse game, rather than a better one. But to instill confidence in the customer and to continue to compliment him or her on what is going well, and at the same time to bring about mini-improvements in the customer's game helps to keep the whole process fun — and the game just keeps on getting more fun all the time.

The customer who started the course depressed rarely left without beaming with joy. "He played like a young god," said the Made in Scotland pro, following behind, with a smile. To continually inspire the customers to a better performance is a gift. To discreetly to keep your distance when the customers want to talk business with one another. That kind of behavior comes naturally to you or not. That is something one could hardly learn.

Made in Scotland is no company, it is a Clan. That is the way it was called five years ago, and that is what it became. A clan is a centuries-old Scottish legacy and the clan feeling is still present everywhere in Scotland. A clan is a family. A family with a family feeling. A good feeling, you want to belong to.

The clan Made in Scotland even has its own tartan, its own Scottish plaid, its own kilt. In this way the men of Made in Scotland created something that was at first a company, but which slowly grew into a family. A family that inspires and generates energy. You want to be part of it. To see how inspiration can be the core of a company is a learning experience, because inspiration rarely gets a chance to play that role.

inspire

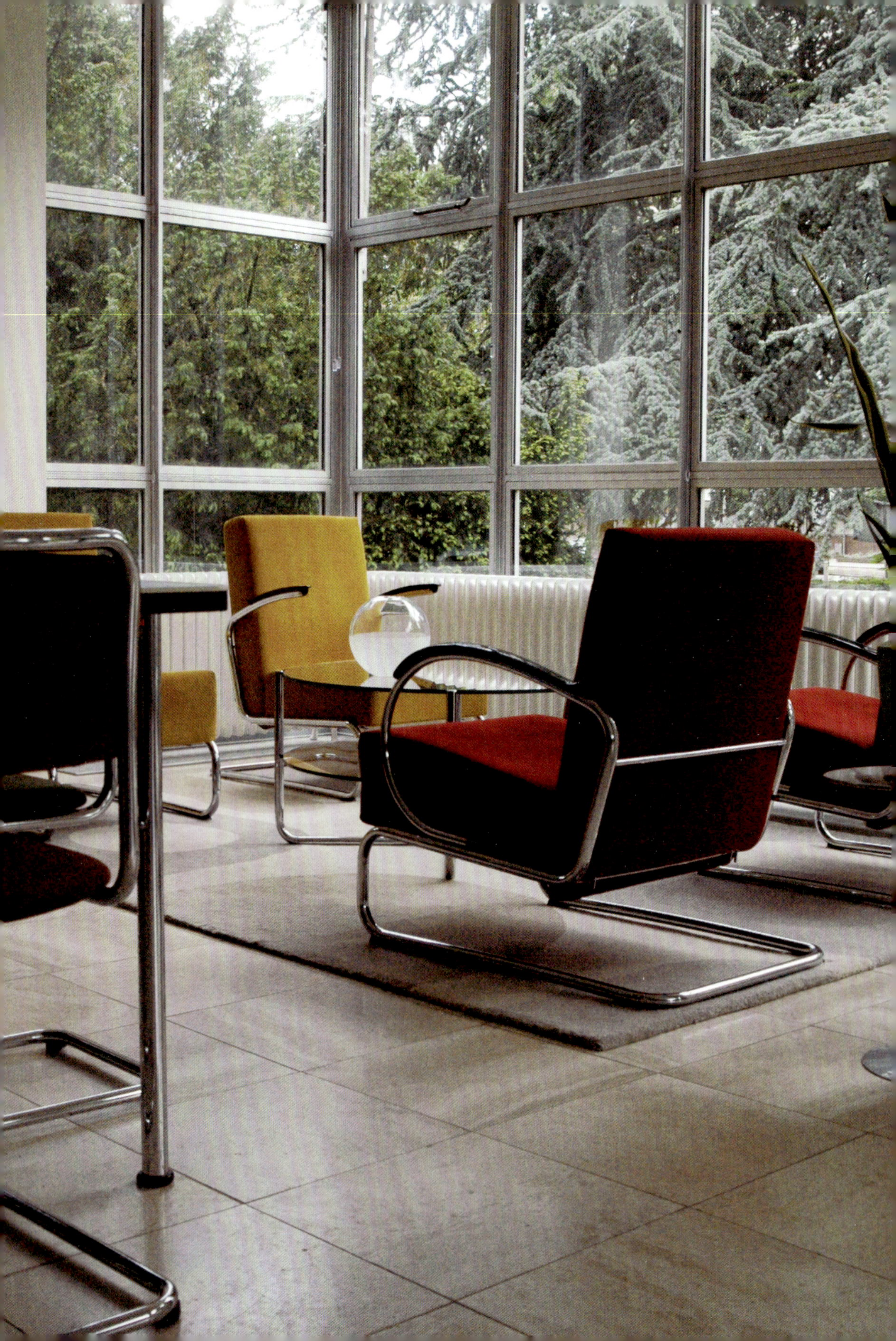

Inspiring Organizations

Why is it that I love being in Silicon Valley or in Dubai? Or why do I enjoy being part of a small enterprising organization so much more than being part of a large, unwieldy organization? The reason is that certain places inspire me. One place will give me energy and another will drain it right out. Recently I was for the umpteenth time in Dubai. Even though, like so many fast expanding countries, they have suffered a setback following the financial crisis they still seem to start a new revolutionary project every week. One is even more enterprising than the next. Nothing is too crazy and everything is possible. As long as it contributes to the higher goal and that is earning money. Now people may have their own ideas about the goal, but what stands out as truly phenomenal is the decisive way in which one tries to reach the goal. Because about ten years ago when Dubai started with the development of grand plans, everyone thought that the people in the small Gulf state were crazy.

Full speed ahead

Take, for example, the offshore island that's shaped like a palm tree —Palm Island. When I spoke with some engineers about that a few years ago, I heard a lot of skepticism. Could it be done? Wouldn't it be better to hold off and do some more testing? How would it affect the ecosystem, the water flow? None of these subjects could be fully researched because the project had to be finished quickly. In the meantime, the homes on Palm Island have been built and people are moving in. The whole project built at a speed that is totally foreign in the native country of the people who built it — Dutchmen. Meanwhile, the Dubainese in record tempo have started to remap the globe in island form. The speed, the enthusiasm to tackle things and then keeping up the energy to bring things to completion, is tremendously inspiring. No messing around with rules and regulations. Cutting the crap and full speed ahead. That is the rule that counts over there and that inspires.

In America, ideas like building an island like that or smaller, or building a golf course, are almost never launched anymore. My guess is that in my own country, the Netherlands, it would take a minimum of ten years before you would have a permit to construct an island in front of our coastline. We could easily surmount that problem, if it wasn't for the fact that we in our country have to keep an eye on everything that's going on around us —what our competitors are up to, for example. I call Dubai an organization. It's a small country, but I think of it as an organization. A country run as an organization. And in comparison, we are a clumsy, bumbling bureaucracy hemmed in by all kinds of rules and regulations. Definitely not inspiring and definitely not a source of energy.

Take a bite

Inspiring organizations and inspiring people or leaders are two different things. Okay, both are inspiring, but it's worth taking a moment to consider whether organizations can be inspiring without leaders who are inspiring. Or that you can have inspiring leaders without the organization being inspiring. The latter is certainly possible. There are many examples of organizations that are absolutely not inspiring, neither for employees nor for customers, but where the leader is inspiring. Maybe they haven't been able to pass on that energy yet. An organization that inspires its customers and the market around it is an interesting phenomenon. Take Apple, for example. That brand name has for many years been able to inspire a large group of people. Also, its present leader inspires his colleagues and employees. Even the logo, the apple with a bite taken out, is based on a deviation of the rules. The struggle against convention.

Take a deep breath for a moment. Inspiring is based on a concept that means "breathing in new life." Inspiring is spurring on to action, it is giving energy, it is making happy, it creates creativity. You want to be part of it. Nothing could be better than inspiring customers for an organization that wants to be successful. Dubai as an organization inspires millions of people from the whole world who want to participate. To go there and to come up with ideas for projects that can then be realized. In an exceptional tempo, new projects follow each other. And Dubai itself is the fountain of inspiration for this. Because the country radiates that there is room for entrepreneurship. That decisions about projects can happen fast. The country inspires. And, as a result, the country reaches its goals. The leader of the Dubai organization is an inspiring man. With an inspiring father. Both men had a grand vision for the future. A clear and powerful story that is easy to understand and that inspires people.

A clear view is not for sale
And now to get back at that story. You can also call it a dream or a vision. What is an organization without a vision? It's nothing, zero, zip. Who or what you want to be in this world, that's what customers want to know and that's what your employees want to know. And thus that storyline has to be established. And carried out in an authentic, credible way by the leader. The leader has a vision, a storyline. With that he inspires his colleagues who, in turn, inspire theirs. In an authentic way, because people quickly and unfailingly sense when a storyline is not genuine. And that inspired organization goes on to inspire its customers. Really touches their customers because it is so completely authentic.

For years, I've found it astonishing that organizations pay big consulting firms to develop a vision for them. Time and again millions of dollars are spent on developing a story, the long-term vision or strategy. Which is then, in an inauthentic way, conveyed to the organization with the help of presentations, videos, and memos. Because the vision was not developed by the organization itself, but outsourced, it is usually not authentic. And it doesn't work. It doesn't **create** emotional response. And all those studies disappear in a drawer somewhere. It would be so easy to put top managers to work themselves, to make them acquire some input, and to develop a vision in which they can believe. And, as a result, will be easy to defend to customers, stakeholders, and at stockholder meetings. To convey your own storyline, your dream to others can be enormously inspiring. And, besides, it's fun and simple to do. But it does take time. Time for reflection, time to think things over. Entrepreneurs like Michael Dell, Bill Gates, Steve Jobs, and Freddie Heineken to mention a few, had a dream and didn't require an outside consultant for that dream. The dream is easy to convey. It stimulates, motivates, and inspires people.

Organizations that fail to inspire have no energy and die automatically. And the way in which they go about preparing for their fiasco is often touchingly uninspiring. It starts like this. Dear Consultant, how can I inspire my customers? It is a ridiculous question. Inspiration can't be bought by the pound. Much simpler: ask customers for direction. That in itself is already an inspiring question.

Even more remarkable is the behavior of organizations that want to re-invent themselves. The whole emphasis is on restructuring the organization and changing the logo. The thinking is, it's the logo that determines how the company is perceived by the market. And how the company is structured and what its procedures are. Because weren't those supposed to be more customer-oriented? Neither cost nor effort is spared to change the logo and the structure. The outside consultants are great at that. But the most important element is forgotten. The element that the customer comes in contact with. The word spells it out: contact. Customers want to have contact, they want to be touched. But that's the very element they cut back on.

Your own story

Appealing to your employees' imagination, offering opportunities, a work environment that people find enjoyable, where cracking jokes and laughter are encouraged — these elements are often regarded as not cost-effective. The very elements with which we breath in new life, with which we really inspire, are frequently forgotten. And so we build an organization with a new structure and a new logo but with the same old uninspired culture. Without a storyline and without authenticity. The story is the central point. The real story that comes from deep within your soul. When the multinational TNT decided to support the World Food Programme of the United Nations, the market regarded that idea with suspicion. Not because they thought it wasn't a good idea, but because people wondered if it was genuine. Or if it was only a p.r. stunt. That's how important authenticity really is.

When we got the assignment to develop for Amsterdam's Schiphol Airport a long-term strategy, we utilized the creativeness of the top management of Schiphol. Our competitor PWC was dropped because they claimed that they had all the available knowledge with which they could develop a phenomenal airport strategy. Our goal was to inspire Schiphol's top management to develop their own strategy. That way it would be genuine and truly their own.

It is impossible for a leader who does not have a story to inspire an organization. Whatever the story may be, it needs to be genuine and authentic in order to inspire.

inspire

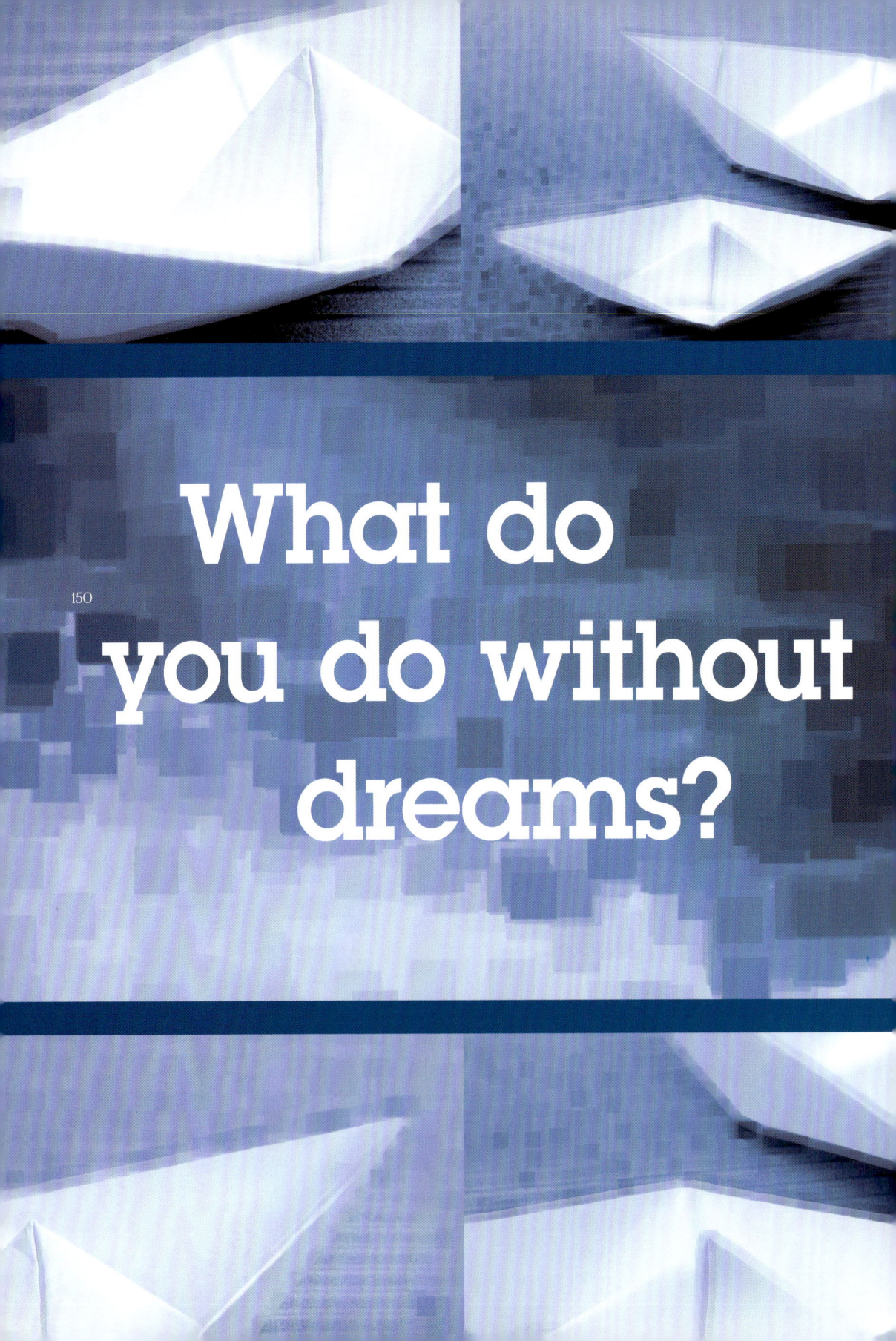

What do you do without dreams?

Everyone dreams. Dreams about things you could accomplish. Dreams of imagining a better world. Dreams that are bigger than life. Dreams are lies, they say, but no one can do without them. Dreams are the fuel of life. What is a night without beautiful dreams? What is life without ideals? Without grand ambitions? No entrepreneur would start without a dream. Without dreams, there could be no entrepreneurs.

Small dreams, big dreams, it doesn't matter. Actually, only big dreams exist. Because a child's dream of winning a tennis championship is no different from a director's dream of reaching the top of his organization. They are the same dreams. The only problem is that often those dreams have disappeared. Reasoned away.

Unknown in depth

Several years ago I spoke with a director of the sales department in a large company. Everyday he visited with customers and spoke about projects, business, and opportunities. But he had never dared to talk to his customer about their dreams. Because why would he? And, besides, it was a ridiculous idea to talk about dreams with a customer. He would lose face, he would be laughed at by that customer. But still. On a certain day, the sun was shining, he was in a cocky mood and he was on his way to a customer. What the hell? he thought. It may be crazy, but I'll give it a shot. And after arriving at the customer's place of business, he blurted out his ridiculous question: "What are your dreams?" The customer wasn't surprised. He didn't blink, but stared in front of him. Then, slowly, a smile formed on his face and he began to tell his story, in a calm, deliberative way. The story of his life, his family, his ambitions, his goals and the future. Once he got started, he couldn't stop. Beaming, he went on and on. It was astonishing. It was energy. It was passion. The top salesman had no idea what was going on because the sensation was entirely new. He was having a real contact with the customer with whom, until that very moment, he had only spoken about his products and services. This was different. This was about something.

Did he sell a lot during that conversation? No, he didn't sell anything, but he created a bond. A bond that would assure that, in the future, he would be in contact with that customer. That he had started a relationship that gave the customer the feeling that, for the first time, he had had a real conversation, one that he would like to repeat many times in the future. It was a break-through moment. It was a success.

The boss of a large multinational tasked me to build up a real relationship with his largest customers. We decided to organize sessions about the

inspire

dreams and ambitions of those customers. A new strategy, in which the main goal would not be sales, but laying the foundation for a long-term relationship. But before we had conducted a single session, the boss's question to me was, Why for heaven's sake would all those customers want to tell me their dreams? To be honest, I couldn't really answer that question.

My dream world

But the explanation of the first example as well as the second question was the same. And the answer is almost too simple for words. The answer is that people love to tell others about their dreams. People have an enormous urge to be able to talk about their dreams. There are so few moments when they can do that. Children who have had a beautiful dream are allowed to tell about it. To their parents, at school, to their friends. And they tell about it with great feeling. As they go along, talking and thinking, they make up a few more details. What a fantastic exercise that is! Telling stories that engage your imagination. Stories that give you the courage and energy to learn and to live.

When does that disappear? From what age do we find it childish to talk about our dreams? Companies, for sure, are not the places any more where we discuss our dreams with each other. There's no money in it. It does not contribute to the profitability of the company. It is not measurable and it is not one of our key performance indicators. Who has ever been asked, during a job interview, what dreams he has? Why would we? We would much rather talk about the résumé and about previous job experiences we have had. To see if we are cut out for the opening. But talking about dreams? No, this is not the place for that. Even though we know that a company is made up of tens or hundreds of thousands of people who all are bringing their dreams with them. Because those dreams are still around, neatly stored away in little cubicles. They still exist. And they have a much greater influence on everyone than the urge for higher positions or greater financial rewards. Because that top executive sitting in his or her corner office with a view of the city and enjoying a top salary is often dreaming away, thinking about his or her children or about that boat or golf stroke. Sometimes those dreams become stronger and he or she wakes up from their daydream and realizes that there is more to life.

Waking up to dream. Or was it dreaming to wake up? Rather the latter. Every one has dreams. You don't need to be the top dog for that. Because even the mailman dreams of a beautiful garden and a happy childhood for his children. Dreams exist on all levels.

I dream that I'm moving mountains

And so we always come back to the same question: Why don't we do something with the dreams? Why don't we allow those people to experience their dreams? Because it doesn't pay? We know that telling dreams brings up passion and energy with everyone. Passion and energy with which we can move mountains in every organization. We come up with all kinds of programs to give people energy, to motivate. We hold pep talks. We organize sessions at ranches or hunting lodges or on island retreats, wherever we can get away from it all. We work very hard to bring energy into the organization. And the most obvious component we don't use. The stories about dreams.

Recently I received a bunch of business cards from a rather small company. On the front, the name of the company was neatly printed, the name of the individual official, and all other relevant details. An exquisite little card. But on the back of each little card there was something very unusual. Every colleague had written on the back a few words summing up his or her passion. Words like Kung Fu, Beer, Alfa Romeo, Bon Jovi, Trees, Ukraine, Wartime Hunger Winter. A simple plan, My mama, and so on. Those were the dreams of these people. And everyone who received such a card and read the backside started a conversation about it. A conversation that was about dreams and ambitions. A conversation that was really about something. Moreover, a conversation that was easy to have and that fun to take part in. Because talking about dreams and passion is easy for everyone. And by distributing those cards, people immediately formed a relationship. Those cards will not easily be forgotten and neither will the people who wrote those words. What a terrific way to convert dreams into energy. Energy that leads to a relationship. Whether that still is about business?

The big challenge is to release or liberate the numerous dreams that live in an organization. Because the freeing of those dreams provides the ground for an energetic company. And the knowledge that dreaming is permitted and valued makes people children again. Makes people happy. It is strange that we have dried up that fountain of energy. That we think that we are crazy if we talk with each other about dreams.

And, besides, having the courage to talk with each other about our dreams brings with it all kinds of effects that we could not have predicted before. Here is an example: I spoke at length with the CEO of a large corporation about his dreams. And, as you might guess, once he got going he couldn't stop. But he did, finally. It had actually been more of a monologue than a conversation, and at the end of it, the CEO, gazing out in front of him, said: "If I listen like this to myself and hear myself talk about what I really want in my life, it looks like I should leave here." I held my breath, because that was a very far-reaching conclusion. Four months after that conversation, I read that the CEO, of his own accord, had resigned.. And had followed his dreams. A courageous step, but the only right one.

Follow your fantasy

How many people don't even permit themselves time to think about their dreams. Thanks to the increasingly frantic pace of our daily work load, there is often no time to think about what life is really about. And it will be gone before you know it. How many people decide at a certain point to make a career first and then, only later, pursue their dream? Because they think that there is no other way. That they don't have enough money to pursue their dreams. And so they set their dreams aside, put them away. For the time being, they tell themselves. But that's a terrible mistake. Every human being has the freedom to make a choice, but thanks to our education and to all kinds of conventions of how life should be led, we think we don't have that freedom. All kinds of misguided ways of thinking work together to convince us that we must store our dreams away for another day.

My father had only one dream and that was walking. Walking in the most beautiful spots all over the world. That was his passion and we were being dragged along everywhere to walk with him. But he had the courage to quit his job at age fifty-three — the father of four college-age kids! — and to become a tour leader for hikes at a minimum salary. And that's exactly it. That's what it is all about. To surrender to your passion, to pursue it, to go wherever your feeling leads you, whatever the cost may be. Not waiting until it is too late. No, do it now.

Dreams, everyone has them. But most dreams are put away. For later. Later when it is too late.

inspire

People who follow their dreams, sparkle. Companies sparkle when the employees sparkle. That is the ultimate corporate dream. So you have to stimulate employees to follow their dreams. Of course, people can (have to!) do that in private, but imagine that people get the opportunity to fulfill work-related dreams.

Surrounded by people who challenge you, with whom you develop and test ideas, motivating goals come into existence by themselves. I described how Google gives people the opportunity to do whatever they want one day a week. Imagine that you combine this and you give employees the possibility one day a week to be in a space with colleagues they want to work with. What would happen? I think that within a very short time, very exciting, creative, and enterprising initiatives would develop that will benefit everyone. Both the motivated colleagues and the company, as well. Time for dreaming and to let the dreams become reality. Only then will the sparkling begin, and you can keep it going.

inspire

Who

has a vision?

To develop a vision takes time, a lot of time. Visionary leaders are a rare breed, and that's why there is so much to do for consultants like McKinsey.

I was present at a directors meeting of a large international software company. All the directors, and there were many, were philosophizing about the budget for the new year. Growth percentages were being exchanged back and forth and customers were being discussed. All rather relaxed. Until one of the directors said he had no idea what all might happen next year. When I said that I did have some idea about that, he laughed out loud. "It's impossible to know what is going to happen next year," he shouted. That was a perplexing experience for me. Of course, we will never be able to predict exactly what is going to happen in the years to come, but we do know the basic ingredients that will determine the general shape of things. And we know this much better now than in the past. The world is getting smaller after all.

What really got to me was the fact that the director led an organization that employed about a thousand people. And they were stuck with a director who truly had no idea. Just as surprising was, that at another time when I spoke with the CEO of a large electronics concern he told me with pride that he himself had no idea about electronics. Imagine a man like that at the stockholders meeting. "Ladies and gentlemen, I thank you for having entrusted me to lead this company, but I really have no clue about nor any

inspire

interest in what we are doing here." That's a basis for trust? A leader has to have in-depth knowledge of the market and has to be able to explain, in clear, specific terms, where his company is headed in the next ten years. That's what we call a vision. Sometimes that vision will cross over into a dream or an ambition.

That a leader without a vision is not inspiring is self-evident. And, it goes without saying, such a leader is stupid. Because with every decision, however small, a leader requires a vision. To have a vision makes it so much easier to come to decisions.

Do pay some attention

To go back to that director of the software company for a moment. In his eyes it was truly impossible to know what was going to happen next year. Take, for example, the company Intel. It produces computer chips. And, believe me, it has a very clear vision of developments that will take place in the next decade. That can be predicted quite easily in their laboratory. Intel isn't the only company that knows with reasonable certainty what's going to happen in the next decade in regard to technological developments. Microsoft knows, as well. And there are quite a lot of companies in the technical field that know where they are going. If you inform yourself and if you are the director of a software company, you will be able to predict quite well what is going to happen. Let alone if you would only have to do that for the next calendar year. In 1996 we knew for sure that the internet was going to play a decisive role in the world. There were profitable companies then already operating in the internet world. But even in 2002, I was asked by a board member of a large publishing company if I thought that there was a single company in the internet sector that made a profit. Had the guy fallen asleep? Was he informed about the world in which his company was going to operate? No. And, lacking a vision, his firm found itself in a lot of trouble. Paying no attention to what is happening in the world, not taking time to contemplate, to look and listen to the world: can lead to a dramatic lack of vision.

Leaders have a responsibility to take a very good look at the world around them. It is not for nothing that they are often called the captain of the ship. He doesn't do the steering himself, but he does decide on the destination and makes decisions in crucial situations. He has an image of where we are going. Looking, listening, and contemplating takes time. A lot of time. It also requires peace, time without stress, to sort out your thoughts. But, most of all, it is a lot of fun. Because looking, listening, and pondering over in which direction your world will develop is very inspiring. During my many visits to Silicon Valley I have always taken something away

— an idea, a logo, a product, a strategy. In short, out of this hyperactive region that is called Silicon Valley, I have always gotten inspired. And that is why I keep on returning to that place. Because Silicon Valley is still a place where the most creative spirits of the world gather. And looking and listening there is always captivating. Sometimes you have to go to such a place without a set plan. Just going there and spending some time can be very helpful. Visions need time to be developed. They don't arrive suddenly, all at once. And, besides, you can never be quite sure when the vision is there. Has arrived.

Birds of a feather

There are many places in the world where the most creative spirits gather, and it's striking that this should be so — that talent gathers in those places. Whether it be dozens of people with talent or hundreds. It is a fact that talent attracts talent. And that the combination of talent and money can work miracles. Talent attracts money and money attracts talent. Over the whole world you hear people talk about whether a Silicon Polder could be established in the Netherlands. Of course, it could be done. Such a place doesn't depend on the weather. But it does have to do with the entrepreneurial climate. And that is not easy to create in a country where the entrepreneurial culture is not always appreciated. Talent heads out for other countries.

At innovative hot spots developing vision goes easier. And so research centers equipped by large multinational corporations in Silicon Valley, and regional offices equipped in Dubai all are ways to maintain contact with the creative centers of the world. To be where the trends are being decided is of fundamental importance. When I started in the end of the nineties with the reorganization of a large software company, people asked me when I would know how it was going to turn out. I answered that I had no clue when our strategy would become clear to me. But that I expected that it would take about three months. That answer seemed reasonably satisfying, but the next question was more difficult; "How do you know whether your vision is the right one?" My answer to that was frightening, because, as I see it, you can never know for sure. But it could be that if your vision does not make sense, the organization will go under. Yes that can happen, if you don't take steps in time. And in history there are countless organizations that have gone bust because of a wrong vision. That will happen.

Are you ready?

Better a wrong vision than no vision at all. Having no vision ends up like an uninspired ship without a rudder. And nobody wants to be on board.

inspire

To develop a vision takes time. Which means giving yourself the time to think about what you see happening all around you and what influence that has on your organization. It is of vital importance. Recently a CEO of a large temp-agency told me that one can quite accurately determine, what shortfalls will show up in the labor market during the next ten years. And where. With this in mind, it's painful to see how few organizations take measures to deal with this. Understandable perhaps, because at this moment the deficits are not yet visible. And so due to a lack of vision you can see in numerous places an attitude of: it remains to be seen. Or even a satisfied, smug attitude. Because organizations that are running smoothly feel no need to do something about a problem which will only pop up in the future.

But that is shameful, isn't it? It is, yes. Shameful. The people involved, the stakeholders at an organization should have gotten much more involved in seeing to it that the company concerned itself with its future. What's the vision? What does it look like? Who developed it? How has it been developed and incorporated in the organization? What efforts does the organization need to take to exist not only now, but also in the future? To what degree are the leaders of the organization taking this task upon themselves? Not by farming out studies to external consultants. No, by going on the road themselves. By personally freeing up the time to look into their own and similar markets. Because it is very educational and also fun to immerse yourself in the story of the survival of Apple and the remarkable switch of Apple from the computer industry to consumer electronics. Many companies are compelled to make such a move.

Who has a vision?

As a visionary leader you need to have sensitivity as well as a strong stomach, an instinct, to be able to lead your organization for a long time. The leader should be the first to detect changes in the market. So the captain can correct his course in time and not only when the ship is about to sink. The way it happens so often. Who is the visionary? That is an equally important question for every organization, just like the question of how big the profits are at this moment. To develop a vision is fun. It generates energy and requires a lot of creativity.

Leadership

or hardship

There are many bosses. And often they are bosses who have been appointed merely to fill a position in a corporate hierarchy. People who are placed in a specific slot in the organizational structure. And those structures are being graphically represented by a so-called rake. The rake means that there is a boss who provides leadership, or should do so, to a number of other people in a hierarchic way. In the same context, one also speaks of a span of control, referring to the number of people one can lead without losing track. Let's assume that there are about ten. Beneath those ten people there's another rake, comprising another group of ten. And you could go on and on in this way, depending on the size of the organization. With ten thousand people, you can easily have four layers of management. And that, of course, also means that if someone in the lowest layer wants to say something to the top boss, he would usually be expected to do that via the management layers. And that usually doesn't work. Even if the message finally does make it up to the top level, it takes a long time before it gets there and a response goes back down again. Usually it is not appreciated when the lowest level tries to directly approach the highest boss. For various reasons. One is that the lower-level bosses don't like to be passed over. Another reason could be that the top boss just doesn't have time to respond individually to tens of thousands of employees. But one can come up with a lot more reasons — both good and bad — that make it undesirable for communication to skip over the management layers.

If you start thinking about the rake structure, several thoughts may come to mind. The first thought that comes to my mind is that it all seems a little archaic. Old-fashioned, out of date, obsolete. This kind of structure was developed centuries ago, when there was a lot of mechanical labor in manufacturing companies. In those days, the hierarchical pattern may have worked well. With bosses, tight lines of communication, and with almost clinically specific descriptions of each worker's function. You don't often come across task descriptions like those anymore. In former days there used to be consulting firms whose only job was to come up with detailed definitions of functions, sometimes including the amount of time a given employee was allowed to spend on it. Those time-labor studies derive from optimum modeling of the processes in the factories, where it was decided how long one was allowed to spend on specific tasks. On that basis very detailed calculations could be drawn up, and it was on the basis of these calculations that detailed administrative systems such as those adopted by management at Philips were formulated. During my studies at the university it took us weeks to study and discuss in detail the system that was developed by Philips.

What does this all have to do with leadership? Not much right now. What it does have to do with is hardship, or at least with the ingredients that often lead to hardship. Still, I would like to go on for a moment to finish making my point, because I want to get around to describing of the most commonly employed way of managing. Namely, managing via hierarchic channels. Keeping everyone in line. The logical fallacy concealed in this is that this usually does not lead automatically to leading, but simply to managing. And managing seldom leads automatically to coaching — another phenomenon of the present day. Every self-respecting manager (and this is even more true in the case of the government than in the business world) has a coach. You are not a real manager if you don't have a coach. Why? Who knows why, but in any case because it seems as if, on some level, one feels insufficiently qualified in one's own field. Is that being a bit harsh? If someone holds a specific function, isn't he or she deemed to be able to do it well? Who can then work together and coach each other. In complete candor.

But all too frequently there is a complete lack of candor in those management teams, or it is in short supply. As a rule, there is little coaching of those in a lower level. Because managers think that they have to manage. And the concept of managing has been framed so that the commands always go in one direction — downward — and the reporting goes in the opposite direction — upward. A form of management in which coaching is built into the system is much better. With which enormous freedom is given to the team members, instead of "subordinates," and where the manager, while coaching them, supports them. Only this way can you develop team members capable of working independently later on. A coaching management comes already very close to leading. Because leading and managing are two totally different concepts.

When emphasis is placed on managing and on the size of the groups or companies to which direction is given, you can end up with some very strange situations. How many people are you leading? is a fre-

inspire

quently asked question that actually doesn't mean a thing. It means that the questioner is looking at quantity, numbers, rather than at significance or level of complexity. We're not talking about the production of Model T Fords, for god's sake. When I was leading a company with around ten thousand employees I was often tempted to resort to the sort of hierarchical behavior previously mentioned. To manage ten thousand people is very difficult. Especially if you think you have all the answers. Or if you think that you don't have the time to coach people and to help them achieve better results. But as soon as you want to tackle the job yourself, your energy drains out of you. The fact of the matter is that managing is really hard work and it requires an immense amount of energy. Talking, talking, and more talking. And therefore no more time for having fun — like dealing with customers.

Many managers find themselves trapped in the role of a tight-leashed form of leadership in which they just hand down orders. That's not what they might call it, but that's what it boils down to. Handing down marching orders. Based on tight, almost unfeasible budgets and in this day and age based on all kinds of rules and regulations and codes of conduct designed to guarantee integrity and transparency. Managing often deteriorates into the dispensing of assignments and the collecting of final results. And if those final results don't tally, we get angry and penalties are drawn up. Penalties and rewards. Carrot and stick, as they often laughingly say. Isn't that really a little bit sad? Is that what makes a manager into a leader…

So let's talk a bit now about leading, since after all that's the subject of this chapter. As I see it, you can't talk about the pure form of inspirational leadership without first, providing a possibly absurdly exaggerated sketch of what the old-fashioned, stolid way of managing looks like. There are people who have that kind of leadership in them, in their genes. People who can inspire large groups and can spur them on into deeds those groups never imagined they could accomplish. They can be politicians, soccer trainers, leaders of youth teams, neighborhood directors. There are leaders at every level. But it is remarkable that one usually doesn't look at a leadership profile when it comes to selecting a top manager. For some positions that might not be so important, but there are situations in which a leadership profile is much more important than a management profile. A company that is about to collapse and whose employees' morale has sunk to a very low point or who have all but given up hope in the company's future stands in need of inspiration. While a smoothly running company has no urgent need for that and can function quite well with a top manager. Who does not necessarily have to inspire, although I think that every top manager has to be able to inspire.

A true leader inspires at all times. Fills an organization with energy, often simply by his or her presence. And that energy, which the leader radiates, can perform miracles. Mandela performed miracles by reshaping a country peacefully. Clinton performed a miracle by not needing to resign after a sex scandal. The Dutch soccer coach Guus Hiddink performed a miracle by making South Korea rise to great heights during the World Soccer Championships. Steve Jobs performed a miracle by making Apple's comeback possible. I could draw up a long list of leaders who, through their boundless energy were able to accomplish miracles.

True leaders guide an organization with energy. And they don't need to hold rigidly onto the hierarchy, onto the "rakes." True leaders often conduct and accomplish much more coaching in their management control. And then, there is often no need for a lot of coaches to keep the surrounding managers on the right path. Leadership often is contagious, which actually answers the question at the same time whether one can learn leadership. Even though for a long time I thought that it was genetically determined, I have by now seen so many examples of people who became leaders, that I think that leadership, to a certain degree, can be learned.

Where do you fit?

Inspire people and giving people energy. They're almost the same thing. When you inspire you give energy. But a leader can also give you a comfortable feeling. A feeling that tells you that you want to follow the leader. So there is a difference between big leaders who can move mountains and small leaders who can bring along small companies. Who radiate trust and integrity and are authentic. And, incidentally, no leaders exist who are not authentic or who lack integrity. Yes, there are people who are in a leadership position and who are not authentic and who have no integrity. But in my definition of the term "leadership," the words that come to mind are energy, inspiration, authenticity, and integrity. Only when these are present can one talk about a true leader. True leaders are few and far between. Managers who put all their energy into pushing their organization ahead, who often feel they are pulling a dead horse — they are often very well-intentioned sufferers. Hardship cases, not examples of leadership.

inspire

The conscious company

On Saturdays my children play soccer. Since I am the team leader, I always stand on the sideline. Often I am also the team sufferer, but lately it hasn't been that bad. I don't stand there by myself. No, parents who come from all sorts of different backgrounds stand there with me. And they all react in their own way to their children playing out there on the field. For instance, a little soccer player does something wrong and somebody yells, "Hey, stupid, can't you look where you're going, goddammit!" Followed by a whole string of swear words. The poor kid will shrink back in his shell and won't be able to play well for the rest of the match. On the other hand, there are parents whose child also doesn't play well, but when the match is over they go up to him and put their arms around his shoulder and say something like, "It wasn't your day today. Why do you think that happened?" Starting a conversation and putting a child at ease. And yet both types of parents had the same need to react to their son's poor performance on the field. One slams him immediately by yelling at him; the other is conscious of what he wants to accomplish. The one is aware of his reflexive response to poor performance but controls his reaction. The other is probably not aware of his reflexes, and gives free rein to his feelings, whether that's helpful or not. The same thing happens in organizations. There are organizations that are aware of their position in the market, of the influence they have and can have, and of the ways in which they deal with their customers. This kind of organization we call a conscious organization.

Does anyone understand the customer?

Organizational structures are put in place to be able to repeatedly and controllably maintain a level of behavior, and it is very difficult to picture "the customer" in the rake. The customer does not exist to a hierarchical organization on paper. Nor, incidentally, does the customer exist in a matrix organization. In that type of organization, there are market departments, call centers, and communication clusters. But there is no place for the customer. On the other hand, there is a place for those who represent the customer in a language that the organization understands. Describing, pigeonholing, giving assignments, and checking to see if the assignment is being carried out; these are the usual methods of trying to get a grip on the unpredictable behavior of the customer. On paper, there are procedures and rules designed to keep the whole business operation under control. As a result, the organization goes about its business in a certain pre-programmed manner, dictated by the CRM systems, rather than by responding to what the customer wants or doesn't want.

Well, so what do you do once you perceive a company as an intelligent source of possibilities? Possibilities that can evolve from a game between who you are and what you can do, together with the customer. You can be sure of one thing: to play the game right, you can't just repeat your behavior. The whole system learns from and reacts to predictable behavior. In which case, the game won't get any livelier. Be aware of what you are doing. Take a look to see that you get everything possible out of the game.

All that waiting time — for sale!

An enjoyable thinking experiment about conscious companies concerns organizations that can gather within their workspace large groups of people. Companies like Northwest Airlines, maybe even the National Football League, which routinely come up with formidable accomplishments. People who work for these companies are often waiting. Waiting in the airport, inside the plane, or, with football, between quarters or during halftime. You can make this waiting time useful by offering something for which at that moment there might be a need. Information, for example. Or entertainment, contact, or communication. It's been estimated that hundreds of millions of travelers' minutes are available per day during public transport. And we are not using all that waiting time. If you play an intelligent game as a conscious company — conscious of who you are and what you can do, in collaboration with the customer — you can easily create new business models that can make a company more sparkling, more creative. Of course, you are the conveyor, but at the same time you are the producer of the waiting time that can, in turn, be sold. What a chance to deal with your own organization in this way!

Conscious companies also take a good look at their place in the chain of values. Of course, they purchase, like every other company. They then process what they have purchased, and sell their products, services, or experiences to their customers. What would happen if you were to arrange your purchasing with those companies that underwrite your way of doing business? And also invest in that collaboration? Many people who now feel that they are not truly involved but only perform supporting work would suddenly come in contact with the business interest for which that work is being done. And this also goes for money spent on the cleaning services. An interesting question to be answered by everyone is: How can you contribute to our goal — satisfied customers? What could I do for you to be able to answer that question in the best possible way? There's no shortage of customers. They're everywhere. You just have to look for them.

Be idle

Under ideal circumstances, a conscious company would consist of an empty center surrounded by a fountain of possibilities comprising what you bring to it and what the customer — the market — brings to it. The art is every time to create an effective, new connection without preconceived notions or standard reflexes that will keep on connecting that which is yours with what is from the others. The first time I observed the empty center that tries to do that was in 1986, when I visited the Tokyo Gas Company. In those days it was called "Empty Center Management." In order to sell more gas in Tokyo, they began to cool the city. They got into climate control via the air conditioners. If you are only empty enough, you don't exclude anything and you see what could happen. If you considered your customers just as important as your own employees (or actually if there is no difference at all between your customers and your employees), what does your use of time looks like in that case?

Customers love it when they are directly involved with the assessments of the companies with which they deal a lot. That's certainly the case when also they notice that their opinion matters. Customers, after all, are just like ordinary people. They like it when their opinions are appreciated. Conscious companies know this and organize customer consultation at all levels of the organization. Then you know for whom and for what you work and who pays your salary. It's that person on the other side of the line, the one you can't find in your own hierarchical organizational structure, the person you actually hardly know: your customer.

Getting a kick out of it

A good friend who is eager to make every company a conscious company gets enthusiastic when he sees that energy is going to flow. That people are starting to shine and that they are happy in their work and are doing things they are good at. What is that, that strange concept "energy"? It's what we all experience when we are doing something that we consider a challenge, and feel we are up to it, and are rested enough to tackle that task. And then it happens suddenly all by itself and the roof lifts off. We are starting to glow with enthusiasm and we feel on top of that moment that we experience. We still are actually just like those children on the soccer field. We want to score. And, if it doesn't work out the first time, there's no daddy around to yell at us and curse us. But a team that helps you to go on. The best way is a team that includes customers. Luckily, we give the child in us the space, and we behave like ourselves and do the best we can. And that is achieving at the highest level in entrepreneur country.

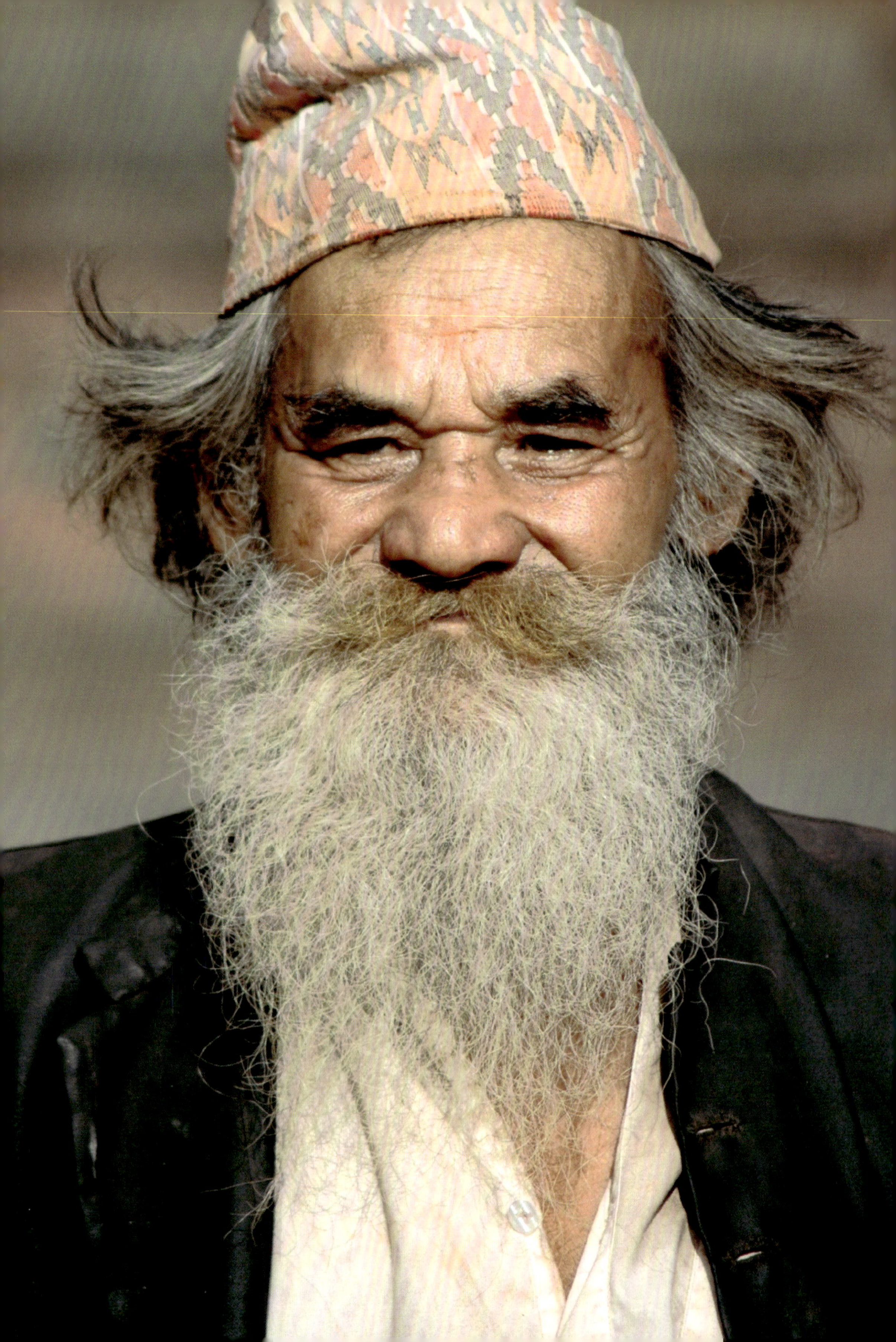

REAL PEOPLE

An executive is standing in front of a group and is telling his story. In the worst-case scenario he or she reads it out loud from a sheet of paper. It's even worse if the script has been developed and written by someone else. To tell a story that comes from the bottom of your heart is very easy. Let someone talk about his greatest passion. Let him tell about his hobby or his child. Or about the sailboat he restored. Or about his picturesque lodge in the mountains. Everyone will respond and come alive if the stories told are truly authentic, if they are genuine.

A lot has been written about "authenticity," but the term is often misunderstood. It seems to be a difficult notion, but it is almost too simple for words. Maybe it's fear of authenticity that leads to the inability to understand. I regard authenticity as one of the most important elements in good management, and authenticity, or genuineness, leads to magnificent organizations. The notion has a lot to do with the search for the core of the matter. Who am I and who do I want to be? Do I know anything about myself—even just a little? The writers Bontje and Kirpenstijn list four qualities of an authentic leader — he would stand for essential virtues, he dares, he is creative, and he has self-knowledge.

Energy balance

Authenticity is clearly frightening. It's frightening to be yourself and to present yourself to others. But the opposite of this fear is the pleasure that comes from the response to authentic behavior. Authentic behavior is rewarded by authentic reactions. What you give is what you get. And that's totally different with phoniness. It's too bad for those people who aren't genuine, who don't dare to show themselves. Because they never enjoy the energetic response that they receive in return. They never enjoy the giving and taking of energy. How often do we deal with managers or leaders who only give energy and don't get anything in return. Yeah, well, we deal much more often with leaders who don't give out any energy at all.

Uninspired leaders are at most average managers. Leadership is a heavy task. Leaders should be able to make their employees open up. How?

inspire

First of all, by talking with them about issues that really matter. By sharing with them issues of vital importance. And these are not the operational questions of work. When I became president of the direction of a large firm, the first day I reported to work I invited all the top members of management for a workday followed by a dinner in an attractive little castle. Everything has to be fun after all, right? And the men arrived with all kinds of folders and files. Full of data about customers, projects, employees and no doubt many more important matters. Even though I had suggested it as a get-acquainted day, everyone had the idea that we had to work very hard. But as soon as I suggested to go a notch higher with the level of abstraction and discuss "why they are working" and "why they are doing what they're doing," it turned out such a discussion had never before taken place in that company. This surprised me again, but then I have been surprised more often. Discussion about matters that are really worthwhile happens a lot less often than you would think.

Who is you?

How in the world is it possible to work openly and honestly in a team if you don't know each other? When you're not sure what motivates and interests the other person, what makes him tick. What makes someone work very hard, what makes him so grumpy, what makes him react the way he reacts? All kind of questions that are worth getting an answer to. What becomes clear is that many people don't really know why they are working. To earn money? To pay off a mortgage? But what are their ambitions, why do they work at all? Why don't they take a tour around the world with their family? Why don't they just do what they really want to do?

In short, why don't most people show their true selves? That's the key to good teamwork, good team building, good leadership, to being a good friend and a good father. Authenticity is important, if not crucial, in all facets of your life. If you tell your child something, do you lie or do you reveal yourself? Do you really open up to your child? If not, then you are still playacting in the most intimate private situation. Because not to be authentic is acting, playacting. And that is very tiring. Because I see so many who for one reason or another do not dare to show themselves, I sometimes call the business world a long play. An exhausting piece of theater that eats up a lot of energy. Instead of living life like a game that radiates energy. Giving energy is something you do yourself, but receiving energy is also something you yourself have to do.

To dare to open yourself up is daunting, frightening, but the reward is large. The reward is openness from others and that makes teamwork a hundred times easier. Management teams that never take the time to come together, and truly spend time together, are doomed to fail. Even though I'm not sure I really believe this story, I heard of a president of the board of directors of one of the world's largest corporations tell how he came up with the idea of going out for a meal from time to time to strengthen the bond with his directors. My immediate reaction, You mean this had never happened before? The appalling reply was, Yes, that's what he meant. It had never, or very rarely, happened And even then it was eating for eating's sake. The way many American managers dine together, because it's the thing to do, but then after a few glasses of Perrier and some boring chitchat, return home at eight in the evening. No interest, no sociability, no authenticity.

An honest answer

Moments of repose, tranquility, like for example a good dinner, are excellent opportunities to discuss subjects of genuine interest with each other. Listening to each other and enjoying each other's stories. To really take in what the other is saying and what they mean. Teambuilding isn't so difficult. It takes courage to expose oneself. Particularly if you have to expose yourself to others who will then not do likewise. The fear of being criticized, of being laughed at, of being regarded as pitiful or full of yourself, a blowhard. Fear for the other's opinion of you. While you know that it shouldn't let it get to you. But that's easier said then done. And yet to overcome that fear is worthwhile. To open yourself up after conquering your fear means there will remain some questions you will have to answer yourself. Because to honestly be able to tell a story about yourself you will have to understand your own inner feelings. And so questions like "why do you work here actually?" are questions you'll have to be able to answer honestly yourself. Because it is very easy to come up with your own beautiful story, one that gives you a lot of pleasure. But, essentially, that would be just another part of the playacting, a role in the theater piece. It is ever so tempting to tell others a story that makes you out to be macho or a story that is very touching in an attempt to come across as authentic.

We were with a group of managers in the French countryside to talk about the so-called business that life is really about. As always, everyone started with an elaborate story about themselves. Those are often very moving and impressive stories. Included in this group was a participant who was telling a story that at first sounded beautiful. But while he was talking my toes were curling. And I could see that some other participants had the same feeling. This was not right…something was wrong here. After he had told his story, you could sense that the group didn't believe him. But it was so beautiful that it made the storyteller believe in it himself. A very strange experience that gives you pause, makes you think. Because how do you know for sure when you really believe in your own story, that it is authentic or not. Are you really the speaker or is your ego the speaker?

Completely unimportant

The answer is not so difficult, and besides a little easier for women then for men. Women have a much better sense for authenticity. Men can be fooled by a terrific story, but, on the whole, women see through the artificiality much quicker.

But it shows, all the more, just how important it is to have self-knowledge at one's disposal. To be able to laugh at yourself, to be able to put things in perspective. Because you are not important, you are not the best, you are not indispensable. You are not immortal. Managers who consider themselves important because they're in charge of large groups of people are often inclined to actually believe that they are important. A feeling that is then wholeheartedly supported by their subordinates. Who owe their positions to the managers, so they have been consciously or unconsciously selected on the basis of their model behavior as subordinates. While every bright and well-trained manager knows the value of being told off, or told where it's at, from time to time. Recognize the value of the employees who dare to voice criticism, dare to be enterprising, and dare to make mistakes.

The ability to put things in perspective, to have some self-knowledge, are essential to being authentic. And, for good measure, I would like to add humor to self-knowledge. A leader with a sense of humor, who dares, who has self-knowledge, and strong values is automatically authentic. It is very nice to work together with authentic people. And what energy it gives!

Authenticity in organizations also has a lot to do with the old saying: "Honesty is the best policy." By dealing in an authentic way as a person and as an organization, you create trust and you transact business in a dependable way. In today's transparent society and industrial environment (think of the Bloggers, who will immediately jump on dishonest business practices!), these are vital values that you can't haggle over. It is almost impossible not to be honest. Because if you are not honest you will quickly be found out. There is nothing as difficult as consistently for a long period of time being dishonest, to assume a pose, to be not authentic. As a character in an Oscar Wilde play said, when asked what her favorite pose was: "I prefer to be natural, but it is such a difficult pose to keep up."

Synchronism

inspire

"Last month I had never heard about it. Now it's everywhere." Is that what you think sometimes? It happens to me all the time. Whether it has to do with a new model of automobile or a game or a style of clothing, whatever. And I wonder about myself: Hey, wait, did it exist already (and do I only now see it) or did it suddenly appear?

You see it in literature, in music, in management theories, actually in everything. In the eighties everyone was suddenly talking about The Tao of Physics (a book by Fritjof Capra), about Madonna, and about Total Quality Management (by the management guru Edward Deming). And you would think that in those days that was the fashion. A trendy product cooked up by clever marketers who were trying to sell books, music, and ways to give advice. But is that really true? Is it true that somewhere there is a dark power which actually dictates our taste — that what we find interesting, beautiful or persuasive? Do we live our own lives or are we being lived?

Provoking each other

It seems to me that the truth lies somewhere in between. Nobody actually orders us to do or choose this or that, but we all order one another. It's more like some kind of energy field which takes care that at a certain point we are all tempted to seek new forms, avenues, and solutions from

stays surprising

the same direction. And the celebrities who ride to the top of these waves are more ephemeral than historians. Not every genius is noticed and not every celebrity is brilliant. The world chooses its representatives whimsically, whenever it suits her. That's how I see it anyway. But how and when do you see an energy field like that originate? And can you call it up?

A short time ago I dropped in with two colleagues who were busy trying to come up with a creative solution for a project that seemed to have got stuck. I knew it was a difficult problem, because several others wracked their brains over it already. When I walked in, I started a conversation about their wives and children, and about what they had done the previous weekend. I only had one short question for the two men. I asked it, and went away again. A good hour later, I had another question and again dropped in. They were in the middle of a lively discussion about a book they had both read. Again, I had a short question, asked it, wondered if

inspire

I should ask how far they had progressed toward working through the problems of their project, but instead I pulled up a chair and sat down and listened to what they were saying about that book After another half hour, one of them suddenly said, "Oh yes, we were going to discuss that project." Then, a moment of silence. After that there was a fast and furious exchange of ideas. Sometimes just short words. A wide variety of jokes in between. And suddenly there was the solution. Just like that. Out of the blue, that's how it seemed. It took less than a quarter of an hour. I was sitting there listening and knew immediately that the solution was the right one.

The unusual thing was not that they had come up with the right solution. Both are highly regarded in their profession, and they had surprised me more than once. What was unusual was the process. A good hour and a half they had been talking about "nothing," and suddenly in a quarter of an hour they were brainstorming like crazy and the solution suddenly popped out. And what is even nicer, this is the way they always worked.

The example indicates how synchronization works in daily life. Both colleagues used their time mostly to arrive at one wavelength. To tune their experiences. To be able to react to each other without any constraints. To combine their energy. And when that common energy was established, a chain reaction followed that was so effective that the solution was achieved within a quarter of an hour. If you ask me for a scientific explanation, I remain silent. But I have noticed that collective creativity increases when one takes time for the energy of the thoughts to become synchronized.

Honesty is the quickest route

To cite another example: we organized a two-day workshop for the direction of a large company. It was a group of at least ten people, and beforehand it hadn't seemed so easy to reach a consensus in such a short time. The goal of the workshop was to develop together a program, and that at the same time, would include our work for the next few months. We were also asked to do something about teambuilding, because the participants had only known each other for a short time. In that workshop we have spent a day and a half on the personal stories of the participants. We got them to talk about their dreams, their ambitions. But also about deeply personal subjects: the loss of a child or partner, doubts about one's own abilities, anger over the unfairness of the world, and the lack of confidence, or courage, and the guts to be yourself. Moving stories to which I could not listen without tears welling up. Human matters that touch the heart. During the final afternoon the program came up for discussion. It was all settled in a flow. With a few important changes and adaptations, but without political manipulations or hidden agendas. In only a few hours we had outlined the work for a whole year.

You could say: no wonder. A cheap trick. Nobody wanted to raise objections after having revealed so much **vulnerability**. But that's not the way it was. Objections were raised to parts of the program, but they were authentic. And honest. And everyone spotted them and could agree with the suggested solutions. And as a result the program was being adapted to those disciplines. In both cases there was enough time to synchronize. To create a sort of energy field in which things are pointed in the same direction. Not being similar but the same. But pointed the same way. And with that synchronization you create the synchronicity needed to come to a new method. I view synchronicity as the circuit of creative energy. As soon as it arrives in one channel, it **streams** towards a natural point. And that is a point that just has to be that way.

Synchronicity derives, then, from personal contact. On the basis of these experiences — and in the meantime many others as well — I regularly organize meetings in a rustic setting. A few directors of different companies take part in these meetings. Telling stories is the most important ingredient in these meetings. Stories about yourself. And of course also about business subjects on the agenda. But invariably in the last instance. And not even ten percent of the time is spent talking about business.

How about doing something

180

What are we doing it for? Working hard, sometimes getting pleasure out of it, happy or angry customers. Sometimes being at home with the kids. And being constantly occupied. Pre-occupied. Day in, day out. It almost looks real. Or is it all just a long play? In which all of us have a specific part or made a part for our self. A part we are playing more or less are playing that role seriously. Let's play, then, because at least we can have that pleasure. Or is there more to it?

for the world?

On the whole, people are searching for a higher goal. It can't only be about getting promoted or getting a higher salary. While all around us the world is slowly but surely going to hell. It 's amazing that there are still people who don't want to face the hard facts. Reality that tells us that the natural resources of the earth are running out. And in this same world there are all kinds of companies totally concentrated on trying to make bigger profits. And bigger profits. And even bigger.

Scraping the bottom of the barrel

A long time ago I knew a company whose founder didn't especially think it was necessary to make a profit. As long as the employees were content. And, of course, as long as that company made a small profit to assure a good future. But that same founder, let's give him a name — E — was deeply concerned with what was happening in the environment in and around that company. And not only in the immediate surroundings of the physical plant, but also the whole environment, the earth. And to that end, he gave money. For example, to the World Watch Institute, a research institute in Washington, D.C., which for years has kept an eye on what's happening worldwide. And which, after all those years of statistical studies, can't avoid the conclusion that we are depleting our resources, coming to an end of them. Are we doing something about that? Not really, although many want to make us think that they are. That's really odd. What sort of self-centered or wishful thinking is behind that? I don't understand it at all. Why are there companies that have to make billions in profits, which they will distribute among people who as a result will get even richer than they are already? Why don't people contribute really serious amounts of money to causes, which in the long run, will — or could — benefit all. But no, apparently that sort of thing is not regarded as belonging to good entrepreneurship. It's still not part of the official rule book drawn up to promote good leadership. If you look at how many companies can really boast of being responsible stewards of the environment, they are damned few.

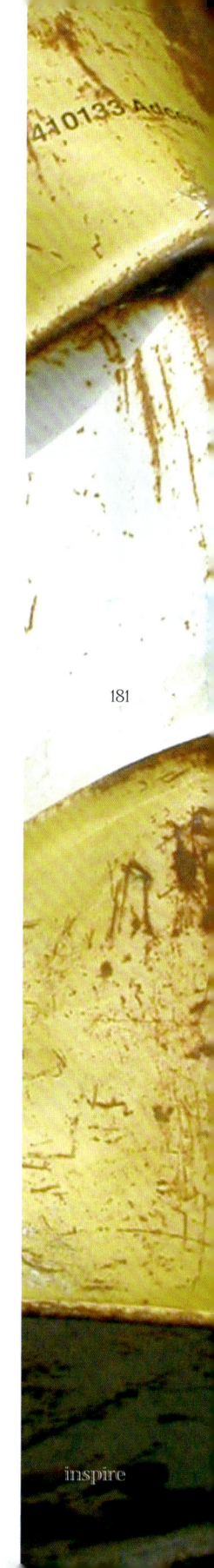

inspire

Admittedly, initiatives are gradually being developed, but there are still many too few of them. Take for example TNT, which gives a contribution to the World Food Programme. According to the media reports, TNT gives about $10 million per year. Partly in services. A super initiative, but a drop in the bucket. Not criticism of TNT. Because at least they are doing something. I sometimes wonder how the shareholders would react to a yearly contribution of $100 million. Would that hurt the stock value or would TNT achieve an irreproachable position? And thereby become a true leader in the world...

Another example. Two people started a company in the clothing business. They ran that from their small house even when it turned out to be successful. Because the profits they made were not spent on building a larger place, a McMansion. No, they gave their profits away to children in countries where children have absolutely nothing. That is a grand deed. Even though it got no mention in the media, nevertheless impressive. Those two people take their responsibilities seriously in a world where it is more and more "everyone for himself and the devil take the hindermost." It's sad to see that, while nowadays there's a lot of talk about socially responsible enterprising, there's so little action to show for it. Because, as with many subjects in this book, what counts is DOING and, even more, DOGGEDNESS. The fifth D! And the most important one. Because it's awful to think what might happen if TNT's profits should dip by a point or two some year. Will the first thing to be cut be the contribution in the World Food Programme?

Never enough

Socially responsible enterprising. One of the many trendy topics of the times. Of course, this trend, too, will be measured and charted. And we will spend countless hours discussing it. But what we are forgetting — and this, I think, is very important — is the whole question of what our employees and our stockholders really think about it. My own hunch is that for most of the employees it is fantastic when an organization takes on a subject head on. The way TNT has done. And talk a lot about it. Talk a whole lot about it. Not because that is advertising which will later be disparaged. No, talk a lot about it, because it will stimulate others to do something as well. How stimulating they are, those great stories. Fun stories. Yes, because that's what they are. It makes you happy, talking about those initiatives taken by companies large and small, and even one-man businesses that are all doing something. Because it is never enough. So let it also be advertising. So be it. That is not a problem for the world. Maybe there'll be a complainer or two, but the world is grateful for every initiative. Take Net4Kids. An initiative that takes care that each contributed euro will end up with the project it was intended for. Where there is no rake-off. And where, besides, you can choose your own project. Fantastic, what a positive energy that gives! Those are the motivators we so often spend so much time looking for. More of them exist than we know. And we are never giving enough, because much more is needed.

Now I am only talking about the things we are doing and we can do to make life for people on this earth a little better. And we are not even talking about the earth itself. We are searching everywhere for that last drop of oil. And oh yes, the reports appear that, fortunately, there is more than enough oil. We don't have to worry. But at the same time the reports appear that the oil statistically will be finished in 50 years. And we blithely build one nuclear power plant after another. No problem. We know all the answers. Because when we are out of oil and water, we can just drink mineral water. No? Isn't that water, too? Oh, yeah. Hm, but we'll figure out a solution for that, too. We just desalinate all the seawater. Yes, to take out the salt. But doesn't that take a lot of energy? That is what we have oil for, right? Or nuclear energy. Very difficult.

This is irresponsible

Take a look at Dubai. It's really a world miracle what's happening there. A desert that suddenly turns green. Fountains everywhere. From the desert sands hundreds of apartment buildings sprout up where subsequently hundreds of thousands of people (they hope) will live. Luckily, they don't drink. They don't use the bathroom and they don't wash themselves either. One simply cannot imagine where all that water should come from. Well, from the sea. Expensive? During my last visit to Dubai I was told in great detail that the only thing that matters there is money. And that investments of less than a billion are no longer taken seriously. Look, that is what it is about. To have and to get even more of what you already have more than enough of. It keeps the mills turning. And the money stays there, where it's no longer needed. Hasn't been for years. But isn't that entrepreneurship? Yes, maybe it is even very successful entrepreneurship, even inspiring entrepreneurship. But it cannot be justified. In this day and age entrepreneurship, the way I would like to define it, cannot be seen separately from involvement with what is happening in and to the world.

And so if we are talking about entrepreneurship I automatically mean responsible entrepreneurship. For many it's not that new. In earlier days there were those small village bakeries that made and sold bread, and also gave free bread to the poor. Why? The baker saw that as his duty in society. A matter of course. What duties do we have left today? A lot of

inspire

laws, but social duties? They belong to a certain feeling of responsibility. A feeling that a baker automatically had, because he was located in the center of society and felt it directly.
At the Japanese company Canon that philosophy is called Kyosei. Which means "spirit of cooperation." To live and to work in balance with your environment. Logical and natural.

But while the companies increased in size and were being led by managers who were totally concentrated on quarterly results, that automatic responsibility feeling has faded, diminished. Several times in this book I have talked about loincloth projects. Projects often small in nature, that like a rag to stop the bleeding are intended to give the impression that an organization genuinely cares about the environment. Read, in your spare time, a yearly report of that World Watch Institute. It won't make you happy. But it will give you a realistic idea of how, statistically, things are going. If you really loose yourself in their reports, you may conclude that the situation is hopeless and can't be changed. But in small ways there is a lot we can do. I am convinced that very many people individually still have the good old feeling for responsibility. People who are willing to do something, who are really willing. They want to give — money as well as time.

The power of attraction

I'll never forget when I was leading the international software company Origin and a female employee came to me with a strange problem. She had about a million dollars in her private bank account. That was not her own money. No, it was money collected through monthly donations from hundreds of employees who worked in that company. With the promise that the company would double the amount. It was called the Third World Fund, by now renamed the World Fund. But the employees had been so enthusiastic that they had had no time yet for setting up a foundation to exercise control over the money. The enthusiastic feelings were too big. So big that there were even people who came to work for Origin because they knew that the company had such a fund. People who wanted to take their responsibility any way they could. Gladly together with others and with the company they worked for. As a result of that initiative, which came from the employees themselves, I have started to believe that at every company, of whatever size, there are many people who want to do more than the things they are doing day in and day out. Who truly want to add value, and not only take it. There is an immense reservoir of unused potential available to do something about the situation in the world. Because even though some irresponsible souls claim that there are sufficient energy sources and sufficient water (not to speak of other matters), still most people don't believe that. And rightly so, because the earth has only limited resources. And they will be finished quickly. So quickly that it is fairly easy to calculate when the end is in sight.

Now then, we've reached the end. We are eager to start an enterprise creatively and we want to inspire in a radiant, energizing way. And knowing that most employees will become highly motivated by being allowed and enabled to add a true contribution to the world. And you know what? Even customers want to join in, because they become inspired by such behavior. And more good news. We can never do enough, so we don't need to quarrel about who will be allowed to do it. We're all allowed! So, let's get with it! There is no end in sight. We only have to do it. We only have to turn the switch. What is stopping us?

AND WHAT NOW?

It can't be done. A book about creativity, entrepreneurship, sparkling, and inspiration, filled with plans, flowcharts, procedures, and hard business instructions. Or can it?

It seems that there are people who want this kind of thing. Who want to hear exactly in what way their organization has to be changed. The most frequently asked question after the first printing of this book was: "Leen, could you tell us exactly how it should be done? Tell what we have to do tomorrow." I've struggled with that question because I find that there are many examples and clues that can get you started. But of course I especially enjoy telling about how companies have improved and I love to give examples. And so, in response to requests by many readers, here are five bonus chapters devoted to answering the question: What now?.

My practical tips and decisive suggestions all derive from the four main themes of this book: creativity, entrepreneurship, sparkling, and inspiration. I also draw upon the feedback from countless lectures and workshops based on my book.

Don't worry. This is not a scientifically based manual, because to my way of thinking that is directly contrary to what you're aiming for — namely, a happier workplace within a happier organization. The central point for anyone who seriously follows up on the inspiration acquired by reading this book is to dare. Because how can people become inspired by reading a book like this and then do nothing with it? The desire is there but nothing happens. What is that?

Luckily, this is a problem for me, too. I want something, but when push comes to shove, I don't dare to do it. I want to tell someone something, but I don't dare. Afraid to hurt someone's feelings or to start a row. The six-month trip around the world that I took recently with my family has changed that attitude. Making my own decisions and, as a result, being more honest with others is now much more fundamentally established in my behaviour. In this connection, I recently held a lecture for a group of directors and top managers from the construction industry. I spoke with them about the situation people can land in when they have presented a good plan to their boss who subsequently rejects it.

and what now?

Without permission

Recognize this? It happens so often that someone believes he or she has a brilliant idea, and works it out and, full of enthusiasm, tells the boss about it — and the boss doesn't have a clue what it's all about and doesn't want to understand it and rejects it out of hand. This is tremendously frustrating for the one who presents it. There are a number of logical or maybe behavioural errors in this process. For starters, the inspired and brilliant plan you have come up with must be so good that you want to realize it, actualize it, bring it into existence yourself. So just do it. Don't ask for permission. But get going with it. It is always better to ask for forgiveness than for permission. And what would be the worst case scenario? Exactly. That it is a failure and that you get fired. And it that so bad? Think about it. You have executed your plan, you are entrepreneurial. Imagine that it will be a success. You can then ask your boss for forgiveness for failing to ask for permission. He will gladly reward you.

Imagine that it is a failure. Well, you made your bed, so now you have to lie in it, but you're the wiser for the experience. And if you get fired, I call it a blessing in disguise. If you find the power within yourself and you dare to determine your own fate, you are way ahead already. If you shoulder the blame instead of trying to blame others for what went wrong, and if you turn your dependent position into an independent one, you will start to work with much more pleasure. Although how many people blame others when something goes wrong? (But they are eager to take credit when things go right.) Start, for example, to point everything toward your own direction; everything that is good and everything that is bad. By making yourself responsible for everything that happens with and to yourself, you will slowly but surely wind up in an independent position.

To become independent from others! At least in your mind. I guarantee you that this will give you a tremendous amount of freedom in your thinking. And you will need that freedom to be able to do all kinds of other things that will be described in these supplementary chapters. Because I can also assure you that daring will be needed here. Entrepreneurs are free thinkers par excellence. For me the big motive behind my entrepreneurship has always been independent thinking. Take care that you land in an independent position. Materially, but especially also immaterially.

We are not at all talking about tips and tricks, but about the groundwork, the foundation — the attitude essential to make this book work for you. And to be able to start working at the hand of this book. And that groundwork has two essential ingredients: independence and daring. Exactly in that same order. Because as soon as you have chosen to accept the blame or credit for all the good and bad things (and as a result you have decided to start thinking and dealing independently) you will then need to dare.

And now we will get moving!

Creativity is the opposite of methodically conducting business. Procedures and rules are the death of organizations. Recently I spoke with someone who had a much better description for this. He said that procedures and rules make an organization congeal. And that's it in a nutshell. Every self-respecting organization, which also wants to be able to adjust to every change in the market, must be flexible. And that's exactly what a congealed organization, perfectly in step, clean-cut and close-shaven and all strapped up with thousands of rules and procedures, is not. I have come to the conclusion that you can only change situations if you go about it rigorously, no holds barred. And to make organizations more creative, I preach anarchy. That is scary! Anarchy doesn't sound promising. But that's where you have to go. To get congealed organizations unstuck from their safe routines you'll have to do crazy things. The safety you always have is that most people have been brought up in a respectable and decent way. So they won't want to do crazy things, because that is not "allowed." Calling up anarchy in an organization is after all much less scary than it at first seems. See the chapter: "Long Live Anarchy!"

And then there is entrepreneurship. People who start up their own company in whatever way, I call entrepreneurs. The motors of the economy or, in other words, the daredevils. But next to that there are also the entrepreneurs within an organization, and I call those the intrapreneurs. Because each organization, for profit or nonprofit, large or small, needs to have its own entrepreneurs. To survive in the long run. Because those entrepreneurs think about turnover instead of costs. Thinking about the outside instead of the inside. And whether you work for the government of for a firm, to consider the outside, the market is of vital importance. That is much more difficult than considering how things will work internally.

Next theme: sparkling. Well, with sparkling it is really going to be fun. Make your own surroundings sparkle. Is that easy or not? We will become pleasantly selfish about that. Let's start with ourselves. Because if we don't find pleasure in our work, our surroundings certainly can't be pleasant. If you yourself walk around totally glum and uninspired, you'll spread your glum mood and lack of sparkle all around the workplace. Cut that out, immediately.

At one point I had to lead a small company that was struggling at that time. One of the rules which that company had introduced, and which has become a dogma in the meantime, was that none of the co-workers could occupy the same workplace throughout their work week. Because that was modern and belonged to the so-called new economy. And so every day management controlled whether you happened to be in a place that you had occupied the day before. And if, by chance, you were, you had to move immediately and sit behind another desk. It was clear that the people who worked in that office every day, didn't get much pleasure out of it. It had become a cold and chilling work environment. It didn't radiate warmth and cozyness. One of my first actions was to furnish a space where I would start to work. I felt comfortable there. Pleasant lighting, a fireplace, a cozy corner with comfortable chairs around it, and a stationary workplace. I felt really good there. But shouldn't I be setting an example? Exactly, start with yourself. I felt excellent and because of that I radiated warmth. Which other employees picked up on. And within a few days one started anew and with pleasure and new energy to work in that once so chilling environment. With cheap furnishings (Ikea) a place was created where people could be and were happy again. Never underestimate the place. A fun workplace, going to it with pleasure…and as a result it will be much more productive. A simple rule and cheap to execute. The workplace sparkles and the people will shine again. Very, very simple.

And then, finally: inspiration. What could I use to inspire people? After I returned from a family trip around the world, it quickly became clear to me that thousands of people were eager to hear how this trip had come into being. How things had gone during that trip and what we had learned from it. Six months just going away. Is that possible? Is that allowed? Isn't that very expensive? That trip around the world has become a synonym for daring. It is a case study, to speak in business lingo, of our need to leave, how we can cut out. And how many people wouldn't love to take off. That doesn't have to involve a six- month-long global journey, not by any means. It could also be just leaving your boss. Or starting up your own company. I have considered our journey as a company. Like an organization, like leaving one's trusted environment. And we too found it a bit scary. Inspiration you get from examples. I call that self-propelling. People who inspire themselves by undertaking things that are fun or challenging will help themselves get ahead.

I was approached by an acquaintance who wanted to start his own business. In the meantime he has started it and everything is going well. His wife told me that he is so enthusiastic that he doesn't know how to stop

and what now?

anymore. Every day he starts filled with good energy. He has a hard time waiting until he can begin again. Too bad that he also needs some sleep. But the energy he comes up with is phenomenal. Completely spinning on his own energy and his own inspiration, he builds up his business. Inspiration is closer than many think.

All right, sometimes to begin you need external inspiration. An inspiring statesman, an inspiring boss, an inspiring book. It can be all kinds of things. But after that you will have to find it within yourself. And when you find it, you will also radiate it. You will become an energy giver instead of an energy taker. And isn't that what you want? In the chapter: "We are going to travel, we are taking off," I try to make clear how you can become inspiring for your surroundings, as a result you can become an energy giver.

Me no guru

But now this. The resistance I found within myself when I felt obliged to write the extra chapters providing Tips comes from the fact that I myself am turned off by the know-it-all gurus who know everything better. Who very often themselves never did it, but who are still very good at telling how it has to be done. That is why I am talking about Tips. Do with it what you want. I don't have the wisdom leased, but I do have clear opinions. And those opinions are based on experience. About how it should and shouldn't be done.

But first and foremost, go your own way. Realizing that independent thinking and daring are the central point. As long as you know that and realize that, everything will be all right. You'll have to make up your own mind. Do it yourself. What do I know…

Long live anarchy!

After the merger of two large insurance companies the man at the top spoke these memorable words: "The company has become a little more hierarchical, there is a bit less freedom." Luckily, he regarded this as a (slight) disadvantage. Because you can find stricter and more severe rules and regulations everywhere these days. Within the business community but also in the government. While at the same time government would like to do away with more and more rules. We are trying to construct some kind of security, with the help of those rules and regulations. A security in which there will be no opportunity for fraud and deceit.

Creativity –
the Tips

First of all, we must realize that most rules originate from a negative view of humanity. While I start with the rule: "Every person is decent until proven otherwise." Besides, we must realize that the only security we achieve through a whole lot of rules and regulations is a phantom security.

Rules, procedures, work schedules, descriptions of functions, and laws are all rather disastrous for creativity. This is no plea for cancelling those rules (although there could be a lot less of them), but I am describing a simple resistance to those rules. Leave the rules alone for the moment, because it's much too hard to get rid of them. But let's start working at dealing with those rules somewhat differently.

Anarchism. Let's look it up in the dictionary. Anarchism is the belief in a society in which there are no rulers. The word "anarchist" describes it even better. "A person who ignores rules, duties, or accepted standards of conduct." That's getting a little closer to what I have in mind. It's also coming closer to the independent thinking that is the signature of entrepreneurial people. Maybe most true entrepreneurs are anarchists deep down. Who knows.

Recently I was asked by a large temp bureau to help bring more creativity and entrepreneurship to their branch managers. As the result of a lack of entrepreneurial thinking, business was falling off. I can easily imagine this happening elsewhere, especially if you bear in mind how undiscriminating temp bureaus are. You know, streets in which you find one temp office next to the other, all in a neat little row. In the same dull premises, all offering the same openings. How they do it is beyond me, but they surely won first prize for dullness. While one thing is sure, in a tight labor market to be able to attract talent, it is you who has to make a difference. So the question that was asked was very legitimate. I started with visiting three branches at random (because all branches were eager to join in with this project) and I discussed creativity and their ideas there with all the employees. The very first thing which was apparent from those talks was that all these people were operating under a tremendous mental blockade. This became clear from comments like: "That is not allowed by the management." "We tried that once and it didn't work." "We have no money in our budget for that." And "I am not that creative". All too familiar, but with thinking like that you will never be creative, and you will never be able to think outside of the box. That will have to be stopped.

Everything is allowed

That's the moment I started thinking about anarchy. Because how could I really tear those employees away from their old world of rules, frustrations, and disappointments? After I had prepped management regarding my anarchistic thoughts, I announced that I would permit everything. Nothing would be forbidden. At first, management did not believe it, but I promised that I would bear the brunt of the anger (if there was any). I decided to remove all the barriers. "Every thing is allowed." "Forget about the cost." "You are very creative." "Yes, do try it again," and so on. I can hear you all thinking: "Yes, but that's going too far!". And: "The chaos you must have created!"

The surprise is that in most organizations people are employed who have been brought up as respectable human beings. Moreover, they have long since been conditioned by the multitude of rules of the organization for which they work. Soon, after about three months on the job, most people don't realize anymore what the rules are — they have been completely integrated. It is not without reason that most bosses make their moves within the first hundred days. It's then that they can still clearly see what is wrong and what should change. That ability will slip away very quickly. So, knowing that you are dealing with decent human beings, you will hardly run a risk by preaching anarchism. People don't just suddenly do crazy things. While that is exactly what you are after!

So it is really necessary to dramatically and in an oversimplified way to allow people to break away from their established patterns. Einstein once pointed out that small changes always leave you with the same problems. Therefore if you really want something different and want to unleash true creativity, you have to forcefully break people of their ingrained habits. There is no other way of doing it.

Every employee I spoke with, and I spoke with many, came up with ten ideas within a week. Good ones and bad ones, all sorts of original ideas. An unprecedented creativity, even from people who had said about themselves that they were not creative. Even more remarkable, they often came up with better innovations. Once again, I brought all the people together, but now at the same time all employees from one branch. All ideas put on the table, to extract ten of them that could and had to be put immediately into practice. Pay attention, important! We were not especially looking at the very best concepts. No, we looked at all those ideas that could be implemented tomorrow. Because then at least we could start immediately. Again, we got objections like: "Is this really allowed by the management?" but in the meantime the enthusiasm was so great that the remark coming from me, "I allow it," was believed. Because ideas that are not realized are nothing. Innovation without successful implementation is nothing.

Creativity –
the Tips

And so from talking to taking action. Premises were being painted, flags designed and hung, and many more actions were being executed that generated a great deal of enthusiasm. And this is not applicable only to short-term actions. The idea is that suddenly employees become integral parts of the organization while they are implementing their ideas, and that they are proud to be allowed to think together. Many of the introduced actions ran counter to the rules that were neatly established in the handbooks. National and international instructions. And the things you come across sometimes! People in offices in the United States describe in detail the way the premises should look in the Netherlands. Talk about a waste of money.

Don't sink back

Why is it so important to immediately go into action and why is it then important to judge ideas on that basis? Because courses, brainstorming sessions, and neatly drawn-up plans rarely result in action. And, as a result, employees quickly sink back into their established routines. So speed is of the essence. And, by speeding, you may overlook some subtle distinctions and may also overlook some very good ideas for the longer term. But do not fall into the trap of getting caught up in subtle distinctions, bottom-line bean-counting, and other factors that will slow you down. Speed is a crucial factor.

Back to the temp bureaus. After the three branches had presented their sometimes wild ideas to all the other branches, a contagious enthusiasm came into being. Everyone wanted to join in: "Gee, if that is allowed, I can come up with some good ideas, as well." The art is that the management at this point creates room for realization with care and tact and doesn't immediately discourage. Because to discourage would nip the creative process in the bud. And, I repeat, no crazy things will happen. Because at this temp agency only respectable people are employed...

To create creativity is really the same as allowing creativity. To begin with, how do you spur on the process? Because to throw it out is much easier. Even more so, often the creative process stops as a result of the mind-boggling rules and regulations. You start a creative process by telling all employees that creativity is crucial for the survival of the organization. And as a leader you have to really mean what you say. Authenticity is very important in that case. You can use posters, newsletters, meetings and all other ways of communicating at your disposal. Explaining what is important, but also emphasizing that everyone can and must join in. Not only the creative departments, but everyone. From the highest ranks to the lowest.

Invite everyone to hand in ten good ideas designed to help the organization increase its volume. Aim creativity to the outside! Because the inside doesn't have much to offer, to put it crudely. It's a lot easier to keep the focus inside, and by most organizations that's the usual direction followed. To look at this a bit more closely: when a company directs its attention internally, the usual result is that people come up with all kinds of ways of economizing, some of which are very useful. And since that's the common practice, I suggest skipping it and directing everything outwardly, to the market. The question being asked to all employees is: "Think of ten ideas through which the turnover can be increased." Or at nonprofit institutions: "Think of ten ideas with which we can improve our relationship with the client."

The advice that goes with it is: forget about limits. Everything is allowed. Rules, procedures, budgets...pay no attention to them. Because people will tackle everything to avoid having to answer the question. And here anarchy pokes its head in around the corner. Leaders and managers must emphasize that everything is allowed. And that's not easy, because in reality everything is not allowed.

But it is necessary that co-workers, colleagues or business partners understand that it is a free-format creative process, with no limits anymore. Because only then will you get really many good ideas. At most, ten people in a group. Otherwise, it will be impossible to follow up on ideas. You will then get a hundred creative solutions, at most. The next step is that you work with the whole group on the ten best. So about ninety will simply be eliminated. But then you also have to select those ideas that can be easily realized in a short time. So you won't be able to select in an academic way, because that will end up in nothing. Select ideas that are simple, that are cheap, and that may even bring in money. And execute those ideas with the utmost dispatch. Even though the rules within the organization will be violated. Difficult to do that, because what will it mean for the company? Well...nothing. By violating the rules with fun and creative ideas, you will create an entrepreneurial spirit. The employees will be thinking; finally we are all allowed to join in again. And in this way you are freeing the organization from its shackles. It is too simple for words. But it is scary because management has to dare. They have to want to do it. Keywords here are: Simple, immediately applicable, cheap, impressive outcome.

Recently I was asked to give some advice about the organizational structure and culture of an electrotechnical company. The entire management had the idea that something was not right. And they saw that quite correctly. The company in question had deteriorated in the last twenty years into the dullest organization in the Netherlands. Horrible, what a lethargic company, with fine procedures, thoughtful management, and scrupulously neat and tidy... you don't want to know about it. Luckily they themselves felt that as well! With the general manager first: Head of the Dullness. And he recognized himself also in that title. Clearly, there was the key to the solution. Significant that the general manager saw this himself. He has resigned in the meantime.

Crazy = fun

But now the solution. How can a company free itself from the stranglehold of dullness? In two days the management was being prepped to consider behaving crazy as fun. Because everybody really enjoys it. We are doing something that is not allowed for a change. Many rules and rusted habits existed in the company. Well, you might say, what's so unusual about that? But the beautiful thing was, in this case, that the entire management, in just two days, decided to break out of that mold. And what's more impressive, they drew up a list of the ten cardinal sins, the ten most important rules of the organization. Because the management came to the conclusion that only by providing examples themselves, by changing their own behavior, could they liberate the company from its historically determined behavior. A day was chosen and a document was drafted. On that historical day the employees would be taken to another location and the whole office would be newly decorated and painted. The workspaces would be completely changed for all employees. Concerning the inside of the place but also the way it looked from the outside. Besides this, the management would start to do things that formerly were not allowed. And then the name of the company was being changed. A total makeover. The shock was terrific, and the support for true change was immediately created.

It seldom happens that an entire management decides to change the course. That a united management wants to steer the company in a creative mode. First release it from the old habits, then start up the creative machine. And you can discern here the following pattern: come up with a way to dislodge the organization from its old pattern. The old congealed pattern that prevents people from daring to be creative. In my eyes, this is the most rigorous method to start up the creative machine; when the whole management starts to show creative anarchistic behaviour...

You can take it for granted that the creative process in most organizations does not exist. And with a creative process I mean a process over all, where all employees are involved. You have to show a lot of strength when you start that kind of process. And be very persuasive, and dispel fears. You have to stimulate, because most people will insist that they are not creative. While they really are. But, after the difficult start, something will happen. At first cautiously, hesitatingly, because people often do not dare. And in that case it is of the utmost importance to let go of the rules for a moment. Just let it happen. Do you dare to do that? Or are you afraid that the company will end up in total chaos?

Scaredy cat! There will be no sign of chaos, because we are so disciplined that we never would or could do very strange things. We've totally lost the knack, left it behind with our youth. Alas. So let go for a moment. Like a good coach of a soccer team. Allow the team in the field to do the work themselves. If you start the creative process in the right manner and the people are getting a start, it will be touch-and-go in the beginning. So you have to give it a chance to let it get started. Allow mistakes to be made in the beginning. Let rules be broken. Notice how people will set their own limits, and don't try to interfere. Allow things to go really a little too far. Above all, steer, if you do any steering, towards practical execution. Because ideas will only be good when they are implemented successfully. Steer in the direction of speed and simplicity — if you need to touch the helm at all, that is.

Scoring successes quickly and quickly communicating them to all other employees. Share the successes, because others will then follow immediately.

C1	Start up the creative machine. With your whole heart in it.
C2	Everyone joins in, because everyone is creative.
C3	Generate ten ideas per person.
C4	Select the ten best per team.
C5	Select on quick feasibility. Preferably tomorrow!
C6	Ignore for the moment all rules.
C7	Communicate the successes.
C8	Relax the rules and be a coach.

Employ the following "Leen's Law": when you stimulate anarchy within a congealed organization, you will ideally attain creativity.

Creativity – the Tips

Entrepreneurship
sometimes

After all, it's your own business

Entrepreneurship exists within an organization and also outside. And take note: if there's anything we need badly today it is independent thinkers. Your own business can mean your own entrepreneurship. But it can also mean that it is all about you. It is your problem…it is in your own interest.

Let's start with entrepreneurship in its purest form: the startup of one's own company. Because when I first got started thinking about this book, I thought it was intended for large and medium-sized organizations that wanted to become a little more pleasant to work for. And, as a result, to make a larger profit. But it's become clear to me that people who have just started their own company or people who just want to start, also draw a lot of inspiration from this book. There are quite a lot of people who are in the process of starting their own company in one way or another. Generally, this starts with having a good idea in which they strongly believe. Dissatisfaction with one's present situation is seldom a good motive. Nor is earning a lot of money. Not that earning a lot of money isn't important, but it doesn't generate much energy. Having a lot of money is great (and I always mention big profits as a measurement of success), but it can never be the ultimate motivation from which you get your daily energy. You get the energy, for example, from the fun you have in closing a deal. Or the development and launching of a new product or a new service.

To gather new ideas from somewhere else in the world and adapting it to meet the needs of your own country is a fairly simple way to start. Copy paste, as it's called. There is nothing wrong with that and nothing to be ashamed of. Just copying. The most successful starters do it in this way. It looks easier than it is, incidentally, because you do have to have an eye for realistic chances. And there always seem to be more chances than you think. Seeing a chance and subsequently copying and importing it isn't as easy as we think. Because several other factors play a role, like: do you have a good network in your home country? Do you have a clue about marketing and sales? Do you have an eye for the social development

Entrepreneurship – some Tips

which will allow you to recognize that a product that is successful in Japan will have no chance to succeed in your county? And many other factors.

The discovery of a real killer app, a true hole in the market, is much more difficult than it looks at first. And many more things will be involved than the technique, or the product alone.

But the core of the matter remains. If you want to start your own business, you will have to have something you truly and deeply believe in. In which you believe in so steadfastly that you are ready to give up everything else for it. Give yourself that test. And I'm not talking here about a one-man-consulting-company (because that is almost the easiest and the safest to start with), but about starting a real company. With people, products, and investments. A lot of daring and faith is needed for that. And time.

Applying passion

Recently I got a call from a boy who for years was busy with his true passion, while making a living at a job. And he felt that the time had arrived to turn that passion into a company. Those are words I believe in. Passion is the ultimate motivation to start a company with. You can tap a lot of energy from that. When he used those words and asked if I would help him, it didn't take me long to make up my mind.

So Tip E1 is: "Where is your passion?" Where is that real dream and true ambition? Where is your source of energy? Because you will need those if you want to persevere.

Tip E2: "How sustainable is your idea?" By all means stop by for a chat with the best and the most critical entrepreneurs. Don't visit too many bureaucrats and bankers. Get your advice from people who have done it already and not from kind friends and acquaintances. Visit the dyed-in-the-wool entrepreneurs. That way you will quickly discover whether your plans are really feasible. And you even have a chance to get some support, financial or mental.

Tip E3: "Offer your resignation and begin". Well, there you go. Shouldn't a business plan be developed first?

As you can see, the first three Tips are fundamentally different from the steps often described in books about entrepreneurship. Because there you have to start with a sound business plan. With a perfect marketing- and financial-policy plan. Impressively structured with many spread sheets and flow charts. And present it to banks and all kinds of other financial institutions. But I don't believe in any of this! Because I know

how important it is to first of all control your own energy source (the passion). And because I know how important it is to dare (to offer your resignation, for instance, because then you will have to do something different).
After that, also the conventional steps will have a turn, but look at John Kao. He had passion, handed in his resignation, rented an empty factory building…And started. And take it from me, John also wrote a sound business plan. But he had already started at that point. And so it is DOING before THINKING. I am a great champion of just starting. Without building up all kinds of securities. But, of course, with a plan in your head. Because your passion is based on that.

Take a look at the intrapreneurs: the entrepreneurs within an organization. Because they are very important. The market-directed, to the outside-directed, to turnover-directed people often think much more independently. Often they also think much more chaotically. But are more valuable precisely because of that. How can you keep within your organization intrapreneurs, or attract them? But, more to the point, how can you stimulate them? Or how can you yourself become entrepreneurial? The key, as I see it, is independent thinking. And with the deep-rooted belief that mistakes are allowed to be made. Because, of course, that's usually not the case. Yes, someone can rightly bring an idea into practice, as long as it ends well. And so beforehand all kind of things will have be done to avoid the risks.

Shit happens

One thing's for certain: with entrepreneurship you can never be totally sure. You can believe in something, you can test it and check it with the most critical entrepreneurs, but you will never be totally sure that everything will go according to plan. Of course, you yourself are convinced of your success. Otherwise you shouldn't even start on it. But even though you are convinced, things could still happen that you didn't anticipate. That's just part of entrepreneurship. And there lies a crucial element for organizations that want to start stimulating intrapreneurship. And so here is Tip E4: "Mistakes can happen." Sometimes people say: "Making mistakes is allowed," but that is not totally correct. You have to fundamentally acknowledge that entrepreneurial ideas can fail. And that it is still good for the organization. Many people have a problem with this. Maybe they should just not venture into starting a business.

Mistakes can occur. When the authorities years ago started Twinning, the object was to stimulate entrepreneurship. But this initiative, which in fact was being led by a couple of true entrepreneurs, was under the supervision of people who were incapable of admitting that something could possibly go wrong: bureaucrats! And did something go wrong at Twinning? You bet. You could have seen that beforehand. Maybe more things went wrong than went well, but even so Twinning stimulated entrepreneurship in a tremendous way. And that was great. But because a few things went wrong, the whole initiative was scrapped. And you see that mechanical reflex at a lot of organizations. There is a remedy for this sort of reflexive response to mistakes. And that is then also Tip E5: you have to place the enterprising activities just outside the regular organizational structure. Because an organization works, after all, according to the way it has been structured. It will immediately apply the existing norms and values when it comes to judging and controlling enterprising ideas and plans. And that is death for all. Be advised: I am not saying here that the existing rules and procedures within the existing organization have to change. On the contrary, let them exist and don't try desperately to create an enterprising atmosphere using rules suitable for a congealed organization. That's doomed to fail. No, make it easy for yourself and place entrepreneurship outside that structure of respectability.

Strict and yet fair

Which brings us to Tip E6: "Treat the intrapreneurs as if they were entrepreneurs." Let them feel, just like true entrepreneurs, how it feels to succeed and to fail. Be tough as nails, just like successful dyed-in-the-wool entrepreneurs are. Be honest and fair. What does that mean? When they fail, the intrapreneurs themselves will suffer as well. Just the way it happens in real life. In the real outside world you can personally go bankrupt. Maybe you don't have to get that low, but if there is no threat from failing, it will all become a board game in which you go to Jail if you don't pass Go.

In the days that I owned Bolesian, we actually never had any losses in the beginning years. We could not afford to, because then we would go bankrupt. We had no sugar daddy or secret financial source. We were totally alone in our responsibilities, because the banks didn't believe in our venture. We had only one real competitor and they were called BSO/AI. A department of the successful software company BSO of Eckart Wintzen. Eckart asked me once why it was that his BSO/AI always operated at a loss and we always made a profit. The answer was simple: we could not afford to operate at a loss, because we would have had it in that case. But the losses of BSA/AI were being taken care of by the mother organization. And, with that, the core of entrepreneurship was being destroyed. And so you deal with intrapreneurs in a rigorous way, the same way the real market would. By the way, that also means that you have to share the profits with them, and generously. Because the market does that as well after all. So when there are enormous profits or successful sales of an entrepreneurial department, the intrapreneurs will profit too, as would be the case in the real world. You can see, it is necessary after all to place the intrapreneurs outside of your organization. Or at least on the edge. Let the intrapreneurs feel that it is their own business. That's what you want, isn't it?

01	Where is the passion?
02	How sustainable is your idea?
03	Give notice and start.
04	Making mistakes can happen.
05	Place your enterprising activities immediately outside of the regular organizational structure.
06	Treat the intrapreneurs as if they are extrapreneurs.

Sparkling in a split second

It's nice that everyone in the Netherlands works in a sparkling organization. Every day you go to it cheerfully and others are saying: "I wish that I could work there". Think about it. Are you working in a sparkling environment? Or are do you wonder why that would really be necessary?

Now, the golden rule is that organizations in which people enjoy working make bigger profits. And we are not going to discuss that point, because if you have any doubt about that simple fact, all is lost. The bitter truth is that, unfortunately, there are very many organizations where every form of sparkling is lacking. Where making the organization a pleasant place to work is not a goal. But where, at the same time, the goal is for example attracting new talent. The solution for that is often being sought in clever recruiting advertisements or creative events that take place in a showroom or the like where they have their initial get-acquainted conversations. Nobody's arguing that those kinds of affairs are creative and fun. But as soon as the talent comes on board, they realize that they've wound up in a mind-numbing organization.

Is it then so difficult to introduce a little sparkling, which would make the company more fun? By no means. On the contrary, it's very easy. With the proviso that you pay attention and understand the importance of that fact. Which brings us, surprisingly quickly, to Tip S1: "Make it a top priority that your organization is fun and sparkling, and let everyone know." But be careful. If you only tell people because I say so (while in reality you think this is all nonsense) then this won't work and you'd be better off not to try.

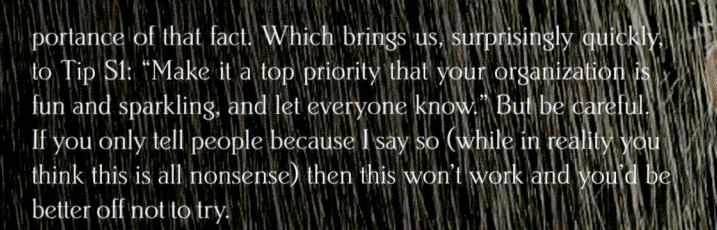

Sparkling has to do with creating fun within an organization. To make it pleasant, to take care that people do their work with pleasure, in an environment that also looks nice. I can already hear you saying, That won't come cheap. Not at all, it is probably even cheaper than the way things are often done at present. Let me explain. To my great surprise, I found that many organizations let themselves be seduced into moving into boringly conventional office buildings. Of course, the first thing they look at is the price per square foot and that has to conform with market prices. That way we are covered when questions are asked by the accountants or the supervisory directors. Next on the program comes the location and after that the interior decoration. Not too luxurious, because that can also lead to boring questions. Speaking about transparency and compliance. Hm, yes, it all looks very good, you could say. Isn't that the way it should be? Doesn't that lead to a sparkling work environment? I can guarantee you that most employees will not be asked to be involved in the choice and decoration of the work spaces. Because that would lead to chaos! Which brings us to Tip S2: "Create a fun work environment, to which people will be happy to come."

One of my companies at one point occupied an old school building. Previously the property of the elementary school of Den Dolder. And cheap... and also fun! Customers went there with pleasure. They even began asking if they could rent the premises for meetings with their own customers! And why? Because they would finally be away from their own dull surroundings. And would be in an inspiring space. Really peculiar. A cheaper property, a lot cheaper, more creative, and more fun. Sparkling.

And a little more about the decor. We did not go to an expensive office-decorating firm but figured that it would be much cheaper to get the chairs and tables from Ikea. Even of better quality (which, as you might expect, professional office decorators will always dispute) and a third of the price. Nicer and cheaper. Wow!

So we have cheap premises, cheaply furnished, attractive for our employees, and of great appeal to our customers. Our work environment becomes actually an asset. And is that only possible with small offices? Not at all. There are lots of large vacant factory buildings and sheds that you could do something with. What you are doing here is getting off the beaten track. And yet not violating any of those precious building codes set by the municipality. To make the work environment sparkle is fun to do, it is very easy to do, and it saves an immense amount of money. And aren't those the things we are eager to see? But pay attention to the fact that you have to slip around those people from the planning board or whatever commission. And it will even go quicker as well.

My experience is that the physical work space for very many people is of a primary concern. The movement to give employees flex time, which gained ground around the year 2000, has shifted over to take into account the amount of energy people derive from their work space. Which all depends on whether the place will actually give energy. And that, of course, is not usually the case. Revitalize the workplace and experience how it can turn into and start to work in a sparkling way.

A sparkling organization also differentiates itself from others. And in a world of scarce talent and where there is a "war for talent," that is not unimportant. Furthermore, we have come to the conclusion that young people are great believers in pleasure at work and in sparkling. Instead of respectability and a tidy pension plan. That change is really amazingly large.

Around the ego

But how can I make my organization sparkling? The answer is inherent in the word "selfishness." Just like the word "anarchy," this word has also a seemingly negative connotation. But, again, here we just have to get through it. Ask yourself what you would like your organization to look like. If you start with yourself, it is often a lot easier than if you start wondering how others see it. Start with yourself and make it the way you want it to be. You will feel comfortable when you do that and you will radiate your feeling. Chances are great that others will also like it better because of you.

Tip S3: "Make it more fun, start with yourself." Describe what you have in mind and execute it. And now for something totally different. How many organizations are still celebrating their successes? Yes, maybe a piece of cake after a takeover or a bottle of champagne at the end of a good year. But how many organizations celebrate each success? And do it in a way that it will encourage others to announce their successes and work to score more successes. One of the companies I was leading imported the so-called Yippee moment. A Yippee is the feeling someone has when he has scored a success. When we started this, the senior employees found it a bit childish, but they too got carried away, thanks to this contagious and sparkling idea. Another company where I used to work did the same thing but in a different form. In the front of the building a large bell hung. Every new order or every new customer was celebrated by ringing the bell. You could hear that throughout the whole building. Everyone got a pleasant feeling when the bell was ringing, and the person who was ringing the bell got the biggest kick out of it. Celebrate all successes with each other in a big way.

Until now we have not touched on the subject of expensive actions. It has to do with attention and pleasure. Because, believe me, I have never yet seen an organization that has a surplus of pleasure. Good news is always allowed. In that connection, too, I have the rule that forbids sending bad news or expressing anger via voicemail or on an sms message. Which Tip is this? S4: "Spread good news far and wide, but if you have any bad news, deliver it only in person. And only to the person for whom it is meant." That will bring a lot of sparkling…

Sparkling – or the total of all kinds of small sparkles put together – will cost little and is simple to do. It is close to you and sometimes so close that you can't even see it. But sparkling will be seen by everyone. Also by your customers. Even better, you can get your customers to be involved in this process.

From inside to the outside

"Extern comes always before intern," is the fifth Tip. Customers are paying our salaries and without customers there is no business. This also applies to the authorities, because without a citizen there can be no taxes, and without taxes no salary. And so a customer always comes first and a customer is always right, even if he isn't. You will tell him he is right. In many organizations, the customer-first position is not firmly adhered to. And internal budget meetings always come first. Or an appointment with your boss always comes before an appointment with your customer. When I was at the helm of Origin, I decided to control the intern/extern rule myself. I would regularly walk into the many meeting rooms and would ask: "Is this meeting intern or extern?" If the meeting was intern, I would pull up a chair and join in to wrap it up. And when it was extern, I would introduce myself to the customer. Who always appreciated this very much, certainly when I would explain why I asked the question. With me it is so ingrained that the following recently happened to me. I urgently needed to talk, as a customer, with the general director of a large corporation and I called his secretary. She said that Mr. Smith was in conference with someone. By accident the question "Intern or extern?" escaped from my mouth. The secretary was so surprised by this question, she immediately answered "intern." "Oh well," I said, "in that case you can disturb him." And she put me through. Later, I explained to her where this curious question came from. She immediately understood and appreciated it. But organizations where the customer is not the central focus would not appreciate it that much. Every self-respecting organization makes the customer the central focus point, but only after all the internal business is done with. The placing of the customer at central stage makes each company sharper, more fun, more adventurous, and more sparkling. For themselves, but especially for the customers.

Humor has a lot to do with sparkling. Humor and putting things in perspective, which is often a form of humor. Humor provides laughter and laughter is sparkling. When you take a look at many organizations, it seems that humor is forbidden. Everything has to be serious and controlled. As if that were professional — that's frequently the reason behind it. A professional organization is one in which everyone knows what he or she has to do and is competent to do that job. But another definition of professionalism is the running of a tightly organized and controlled organization. Starting from a negative view of humanity, a suspicious organization is created in which humor and putting things in perspective are seen as weakness. The organization then turns into another of those previously mentioned congealed organizations.

As leader of a large company, I decided to pull the following April Fool's joke. In the early morning hours of April 1 in the elevator of our headquarters, I placed a small desk and a chair. Added a small chair and spent a couple of hours there. Every employee or groups of employees who stepped in the elevator, encountered a working general director. That was weird and for months it was spoken about. Sometimes I would invite employees to take a seat and we would have a short talk. Was very appreciated. To give an indication that I also as highest boss could do crazy things and wasn't as important as it sometimes seemed. Because a lot of leaders truly believe that they are very important. And suddenly they will be serious and show a different behavior. Strange, isn't it?

Tip S6: "Managers are not more important than all the others and they must set an example by putting things in perspective and by their sense of humor." What I have noticed is that the best CEOs I know often have a sense of humor and the ability to see things in their proper context. The imitation bosses don't have that and hold on tightly to an image that does not make any sense. Managers with a sense of humor and an ability to see things in perspective are at the basis of sparkling. Doing strange, unexpected things is soon seen as humorous.

Look for a showpiece

Next to humor, pride is also an important element of sparkling. A company whose employees are proud sparkles more than a company for which they are ashamed to be working. Talking enthusiastically about your company at a birthday party, for example, sparkles and the sparkling radiates out to the listeners. Instead of badmouthing your company in great detail. Pride is something you have to build up. Communication and marketing have to be pointed into that direction, as well. TNT is proud of the support it gives to the World Food Programme. Employees talk about it with great pride, and over the years the market has also started to appreciate it enormously. Name recognition connected to a deeper value can also make people feel proud of an organization. So that the organization becomes proud of itself. ING sponsors Formula 1; which doubtless will enhance the company's name recognition, but it doesn't go much deeper than that. The wide name recognition isn't linked to a value that will help improve conditions in the world. And that's a pity when so much money is spent on such sponsorships. Because all the employees also see the campaigns. This is often forgotten, because, hey, isn't this all about name recognition? And the employees already know the name. While it is clear that all campaigns could contribute to the pride of the company. Sparkling being the result. Tip S7: "Take care that your organization radiates pride. So you have to take care that there is something to be really proud of!"

Sparkling is made up out of numerous small sparkles. The way a diamond is made of numerous twinkling facets. You have to view sparkling the same way. It is the total sum of all the beautifully cut facets that allow the diamond to twinkle. And it is the total sum of all the small fun things that let the organization sparkle. So there is a lot you have to do, but they are all small things. Small steps. And when you are dealing with a dull organization, it is not that difficult to bring in some sparkling. But, afterwards, you can continue with this endlessly. That is why the Tips in this chapter are only a very small number of all the things you can do. Once you get the taste for it, you can add many more yourself. And within a short time you will have a much nicer, more sparkling organization.

S1	Make it a priority that your organization is fun and sparkles and tell everyone.
S2	Create a fun work atmosphere where people are eager to be.
S3	Make it more fun, start with yourself.
S4	Spread good news far and wide, but communicate bad news only personally. To the person for whom it is meant.
S5	Extern always comes before intern.
S6	Managers are not more important than all the others, and they have to be an example by keeping things in perspective and by their sense of humor.
S7	Take care that your organization radiates pride. Take care that something is present to be really proud of.

We're going to travel

...

To Inspire –
The Tips

To inspire: everyone knows what that is. Everyone has something that they have come across that inspires him or her. It could be a book, a person, a company, or a certain environment. You will feel it immediately. And so when I was contemplating the chapter about inspiration, I really couldn't come up with anything else than the metaphor of the world tour I recently made with my wife and my children. That is about something that seems to inspire a lot of people, but it also is about the daring required to let go. To let go, to take off. Not fleeing from something, but taking yourself along. In this whole book I've often pointed out how important it is to choose for yourself. But I've also emphasized how difficult that is. There are many books about daring and even doing, but they don't make doing and daring any easier. You need inspiration to do it. That is why this chapter starts with the world tour.

For many years we had wanted to take off for a longer period of time. To show our children that the world is bigger than only the Netherlands. But also to show them how fortunate we are here. And to broaden their standards and values in this way. To let them feel that the discussions we have in the Netherlands about important matters actually often are not important. That in the world there are people of all colors and all races. And that those people are mostly poorer than we are. To show that the Netherlands is a very clean country in comparison with the rest of the world. To experience nature, which will be changed in fifty years. To show how other parts of the world are being polluted. But also to experience how beautiful the rest of the world is. In short, to give them — but also ourselves — an experience that will decide the course of your life. Because when I myself was seventeen years old and I went for a year to the United States, it was an experience that determined the whole rest of my life. But when do you leave then? And how is it going to be paid for? And will you hand in your resignation? Are the children allowed to take off from school? And how do you plan all this?

Be committed

Questions, questions, questions that often lead to not traveling at all. Because the easiest thing to do is not to go at all. Reasons for not going are easy to come up with. To keep ourselves from procrastinating, we decided in January 2007 that we would leave in June of that same year. Will you have enough time to plan everything? No, but the pressure is so great that you don't have time to change your mind. Because you know that when you tell the headmaster of the elementary school that you are going to leave in June, you are really obliged to go. Put yourself under unreasonable pressure and make the timeline really unrealistically short. You will be so busy with organizing that there'll be no time left to change your mind. Because, before you know it, you are talking with a senior education official and you truly cannot go back. You hand in your resignation as of June and then you are stuck. You will suddenly have to leave, whether you like it or not. Did we wonder, after doing this, whether our decision to go away was the right one? Of course, quite often in fact. But, in the meantime, we were very busy with the preparations and we quickly forgot about our doubts. Because we had to spend the night somewhere in Peru. A much more pressing problem.

And that's the same with everything in this book. Many things are so scary to do that you should not spend much time thinking about them. To put ourselves under even more pressure, we came up with many more things and, as a result, we could not change our mind. (there was no road back). We decided to make a book about the tour and found a publisher. And via the publisher a conversation started with National Geographic Junior to make twelve extra digital editions about the twelve countries we would visit during this trip. We looked for sponsors for these extra editions and so it had to continue. We were just committed to the trip. There was no turning back. Finally, we concocted together with Nemo (an educational attraction in Amsterdam where in a playful way you get acquainted with a world full of knowledge and technology) an exibition and we even found some sponsors for this. It started really to look like a small organization. Which made me feel at home, of course. We came up with a name, the Travelkids Expedition. And because the Netherlands travel bureau SNP owned the name Travelkids, we also received a strong link with them. Within three months a small company was erected, our world tour, which had been named: Travelkids Expedition.

"Yes, I could do that too if I had a lot of money." That's also an often-heard excuse to not go. With five people three weeks in Costa Rica will cost about 4,000 Euros. Per person? No, for the whole gang. The better you want to explore a country, the closer you have to be to the people and thus the cheaper the trip will be. A ticket around the world, all air travel combined: about 2,000 Euros per person. I agree, it is not all for free. But instead of building a new kitchen in your house, you could be well on your way. Keep your old car and there you go. So all that is not a problem.

Not everyone can afford this, but neither is it very exclusive. By all means, avoid staying in expensive hotels and resorts, because then it will be prohibitive and you won't really see the character of the countries you visit. Every resort is the same. All equally beautiful and none of them representative of the world. The most difficult is saying goodbye to your job. Because what will happen when you return? Well, then you just start up with something much more fun. Didn't you always want to leave the position you were in? But that security. That phantom security keeps you from it.

Back from the trip we are doing fun things again. We are working again, but now in a place that is more fun. We are actually earning more. We have had an unforgettable time with the kids. Because which family has ever been together night and day for six months? Twenty four hours a day. Doing everything together. During our trip, my father suddenly died and that made me realize that every day is important. How many people plan the most fantastic ambitious businesses — and then oh, well, we'll do that later. We have had the gift of being together for six months and it will always set the course of our lives. The children have been changed without noticing this themselves. It was very good.

I have discovered that our world tour, when I talk about it, inspires many people. At first, I thought that it was inspiring people to take a world tour. But I had that wrong, because it actually inspires people to do what they really want to do. It inspires people to inspire themselves. That sounds good!

How do you handle inspiration within your own organization? A little bit the same way as with such a dream trip. First of all, inspiration is important. I can't imagine a manager who is not able to inspire. What does that manager do? Managing? What is that? Organizing so that everything runs according to procedure. No, managing is taking care that the organization has enough energy and that it is able to hold on to that energy. Managers inspire their employees to achieve beautiful things. They help their employees elevate themselves. And in this way they build up whole organizations that inspire. First inspire the employees and after that the customers, as well. Because an inspired and energetic organization inspires the customers, too. And that ultimate feeling is what you want to reach.

The tour around the world had the remarkable sequence of first DOING and then only THINKING. That gives a lot more energy than first to think over a subject to bits and pieces. In most organizations we have by now already put in so much thought that we should at this point first start with doing. Doing inspires more than thinking. Tip I1: "From where do you get your inspiration?" A good question to start off with. The thought about our trip alone was inspiring. But the doing, the planning and organizing of the trip was many times more inspiring.

Tip 12:"So as soon as you know where your inspiration will come from, you should immediately put it into action." Because inspiration starts with yourself. Whether you are the manager or not.

Nicely important?

My little daugher once asked me who or what are important people? People with a lot of money? Or were they people who were the boss of a country. Seems an easy question... I am reminded of this because during our world tour we visited projects where poor children were being helped by volunteers, like a street children's project in Ecuador, and an education project for kindergartners in Peru. High up in the mountains, far away from everybody. Those children were without anything. No parents, no clothes, no food, no love. Our children saw this immediately and it made a deep impression. "Look at that, those children are walking barefoot."

In Peru we were led around for a day in the Andes at an elevation of about 4,500 meters. The manager of a large kindergarten education project gave us a tour and showed us the little schools they had built. For many years he had worked with those children, who were located so far away from the authorities the capital, Lima, so that they had just been forgotten. Literally! What a special day. That man, Walter, was an important man. I could immediately explain that to my children. Walter was important for those thousands of small children. No Walter, no education. And so no future. That was really an important man. Life-saving important. To me he was an exceptionally inspiring man, who had put aside his own prosperity for the well being of thousands of children. You don't have to look for inspiring people among famous high-placed people. Inspiring people are to be found on every level. People who with their passion really add something substantial to the world. That is inspiring!

People tap energy from being allowed to follow their dreams and ambitions. Because everyone has energy inside with which he or she can inspire him or herself. And that is what you want to tap as an organization. To get back to Tip 11, the searching for your inspiration. The easiest way is to look for it within yourself. Of course, you can find it in people or other things outside yourself, but when you find the inspiration within yourself you will then also tap your own energy source. For example, for years I had wanted to make that trip around the world. The taking on and the execution of that dream always gives energy. Or for a long time I have wanted to organize walking tours. To then immediately start with it and print some brochures to announce the sale of those tours gives an enormous amount of energy. Is that energy the same thing as inspiration?

I think so. In any case, it is the same energy you get when you are being inspired by an external source. The difference is that it now comes from within yourself. And when you are so inspired while working, you will also radiate energy out onto your environment. You are now starting to inspire others. That's the way it also worked with that world tour.

The immediate transformation into deeds (Tip 12), the immediate doing, can be introduced in an organization in the following way. Every person has dreams and ambitions. Put aside or forgotten, perhaps, but still always present. And that can turn into large dreams like "I want to become prime minister or president," or into small ones like "At some point in my life I want to bake a cake." And once you know that everyone has those dreams, ask them to describe them. Ask your employees to write or tell something about their dreams. Create an internal document in which each employee, or from all employees in your team, the individual's dreams or ambitions are described. Hire a journalist who interviews every employee and can put all the dreams and ambitions on paper. In short, make an inventory of the dreams. Share them with each other. What will happen? Every person likes to talk about his or her dreams. That gives energy. Even though it might not have any connection with the immediate work environment. Other people generally enjoy hearing such inspiring stories. Once a year a conference is being held in Zeist with the name PINC. That stands for People, Inspiration, Nature, and Creativity. For a whole day, people share their inspiring stories, which always have to do with dreams and ambitions. Filled with energy, the visitors leave at the end of the day from the conference. You should go there sometime. Compare that with the numerous conferences you attend where, after the first half hour, you think: "What am I doing here, for godssake?"

Back to inspiration, Tip 13: "Make an inventory of all dreams and ambitions within your organization and talk about it." And, of course, there is another step that goes with it. And that is that you want to explore how all those dreams and ambitions can have a greater effect on your own organization. I must admit that they have done that already if you make an inventory and you share it. Because energy gives off energy. But go one step further and you will get to Tip 14:"Collect all of your dreams and ambitions that have to do with work and implement them." In that case what you do first is tap the energy, to bring up the peoples' inspiration. But then give your consent to really let them do something with it within their work environment. Then you will see something happening! You are directing the inspiration located within the people onto their own organization. You will tap a tremendous source of energy which, until now, has been untouched.

Inspire yourself

You have now done two things already. Tips I1 and I2 concern yourself. Energize yourself. That's the basis, the foundation. In Tip I3 and I4 you are in effect doing it with your whole organization. Gather the energy sources and tap into them. As you can see, we haven't even touched on the energy from the outside. Everything is still coming from the inside. Besides, it is a great deal cheaper than hiring expensive speakers who will have to inspire from the outside. You just do it yourself.

I always wanted to develop a program to give Tip I4 a permanent character. Not with an idea box, because people will put an idea in it which then has to be judged by others. No, let people start themselves. Leave time for that, give people the opportunity to present their dreams and ambitions and give them the freedom to bring those ambitions that fit with the company a step further. At Google they call that Pursue Your Dreams. Inspiration, the energy source you will need to accomplish big things. If you happen to be the kind of manager who cannot inspire, then in that case you can use such a program. Because along with that, people inspire themselves.

I1	From where do you get your inspiration?
I2	Turn this inspiration as soon as you know where it comes from, immediately into deeds.
I3	Make an inventory of all dreams and ambitions that are alive within your organization and talk about it.
I4	Collect all dreams and ambitions and implement them.

AND THANKS

How do you reach the point where you finally put all those ideas about creativity, entrepreneurship, sparkling, and inspiring down on paper? Where do all those ideas come from? When you start to think about, you want to thank everyone who has something to do with it.

When I finished high school my parents sent me to the United States. For a year. To become more self-sufficient after having grown up in a sheltered environment. That worked out pretty well. Staying for a year in that enormously enterprising country has determined everything that I undertook afterwards. My thinking about enterprising, taking risks, and creating was largely formed in the United States.

Contrary to everything that I've written here about enjoying, I have neglected my wife and children shamefully. Because, well, aside from writing I also had to run a few companies. But even though I could spend less time with my family in that period, the writing process has had a very special effect on the children in the Zevenbergen home. First the oldest, then the middle child, and finally the youngest started enthusiastically on a book. In the meantime, dozens of books and pamphlets have seen print. Creativity flourishes wherever it is stimulated by an example...

Helping me to think things out thoroughly and to get my thoughts in order, there were many who were thinking along similar lines as mine and a few who even collaborated on sections with me. Peter Weijland, one of the innovative thinkers at Escador (one of my companies), made a significant contribution to this book by giving me notes on substance and style. Thanks for that. Other contributions from Escador came from Theo van den Brink and my good friend Alfred Schmits.

Dirk Jasper, one of the most optimistic entrepreneurs I know and also a good friend, was enthusiastic from day one. Accepting all the risks that go with providing such support, he rounded up all kinds of people to make sure that this book would sparkle and inspire. Thanks Dirk, for your energy and your inspiration with which you have given shape to the production of this book. And from the very start, he put his team to work, among others Marcel, Katja, Frans, Peter, Hans, and Maarten. Many thanks to all of you.

Bram Donkers turned my text, which I had jotted down in raw form on paper, into readable and exciting sentences. And a coherent story. How much work that must have been! But, luckily, he also got into a flow...

BOOKS CONSULTED

1. *The Business of Innovation,*
   by Roger Bean and Russell Radford, AMACOM 2001
2. *Authentiek leiderschap,*
   by Johan Bontje, Jan Willem Kirpestijn, and Willem Vreeswijk, Utrecht 2005.
3. *Finite and Infinite games: A Vision of Life as Play and Possibilities,*
   by James P. Carse Ballantine Books, USA 1987.
4. *The Innovator's Dilemma,*
   by Clayton M. Christensen, Harvard Business School Press, USA 1997.
5. *Flow, psychologie van de optimale ervaring,*
   by Mihaly Csikszentmihalyi, John H. Boom, 1999.
6. *Creativiteit, over flow, schepping en ontdekking,*
   by Mihaly Csikszentmihalyi, John H. Boom, 1998.
7. *De weg naar flow,*
   by Mihaly Csikszentmihalyi, John H. Boom, 1999.
8. *De 8ste eigenschap; van effectiviteit naar inspiratie,*
   by Stephen Covey, Business Contact, Amsterdam 2005.
9. *Inspiration,*
   by Wayne W. Dyer, UK 2005.
10. *The Rise of the Creative Class,*
    by Richard Florida, The Perseus Books Group, USA 2004
11. *The Living Company,*
    by Arie de Geus, Nicholas Brealey Publishing, UK 1999.
12. *The Birth of the Chaordic Age,*
    by Dee Hock, Berrett-Koehler Publishers, USA 1999.
13. *Slow,*
    by Carl Honoré, Lemniscaat, Rotterdam 2004
14. *The Play Ethic,*
    by Pat Kane, Pan Macmillan, UK 2004.

15. *The World Café,*
    by David Isaacs and Juanita Brown, Berrett-Koehler Publishers; 2005
16. *The Dream Society,*
    by Rolf Jensen, McGraw-Hill; 2001.
17. *Het geluk; een handleiding,*
    by Manfred Kets de Vries, Nieuwezijds bv, Amsterdam 2003.
18. *Visions,*
    by Michio Kaku, Oxford University Press, UK 1999.
19. *Jamming,*
    by John Kao, HarperCollins Publishers, UK 1997.
20. *Fish Tales,*
    by Stephen C. Lundin, Hodder & Stoughton General Division, UK 2003.
21. *Bezielde kosmos,*
    by Ervin Laszlo, Uitgeverij Ankh-Hermes, Deventer 2005.
22. *Evolutionair leiderschap,*
    by Peter Merry, Gottmer Uitgevers Groep bv, Haarlem 2006.
23. *Presence, Exploring Profound Change in People, Organizations and Society,* by Peter Senge, Joseph Jaworski, C. Otto Scharmer, and Betty Sue Flowers, Doubleday Business 2005.
24. *Een nieuwe aarde, de uitdaging van deze tijd,*
    by Eckhart Tolle, Uitgeverij Ankh-Hermes, Deventer 2005.
25. *Managing to Have Fun,*
    by Matt Weinstein, Simon & Schuster Books, USA 1997.
26. *iCon, Steve Job: The Greatest Second Act in the History of Business,*
    by Jeffrey S. Young, Wiley, USA 2005.
27. *Create Your Future,*
    by Leen Zevenbergen, RCC Apeldoorn, 1996

COLO-FON

Final editing:
Bram Donkers

Translating:
Marianne Swan

Design and production:
Barnyard - Marcel Boshuizen, Katja Kamphoff, Frans Mooren, Peter Schlumpf, Hans Felix, Maarten Uilenbroek, Dirk Jasper

Contributions from:
Theo van den Brink, Alfred Schmits, Peter Weijland